Collins
gem

Watercolour Tips

T0025369

Practical tips to start you painting

Ian King

First published in 2004 by
Collins, an imprint of
HarperCollins*Publishers*
1 London Bridge Street, London, SE1 9GF

This edition published 2012

HarperCollins*Publishers*
Macken House, 39/40 Mayor Street Upper
Dublin 1, D01 C9W8, Ireland

The Collins website address is: www.collins.co.uk

Collins Gem® is a registered trademark of
HarperCollins Publishers Limited.

17

A catalogue record for this book is available from the British Library

Created by: SP Creative Design
Editor: Heather Thomas
Designer: Rolando Ugolini
Photographer: Charlie Colmer

Based on material from Ian King's *Watercolour Landscape Techniques*.

Artwork reproduced by kind permission of Anglia Television:
pages 9, 81, 87, 97, 100, 108, 109, 121 and 136
ISBN-13 978 0 00 717708 0

Colour reproduction by Digital Imaging
Printed and bound in Malaysia

MIX
Paper | Supporting
responsible forestry

FSC
www.fsc.org

FSC™ C007454

CONTENTS

ABOUT THE AUTHOR

Ian King is known to millions through his popular television series *King and Country*. In this book, he shares his vast wealth of knowledge and experience with you. His unique teaching methods and seven-stage system have helped hundreds of people to become more confident about painting in watercolours and produce successful paintings.

Ian's striking watercolours look detailed at first glance but closer investigation reveals a simple, almost

The Crescent, Wisbech
38 x 56 cm (15 x 22 in)

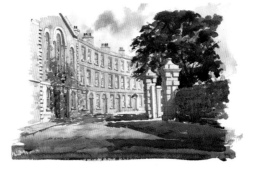

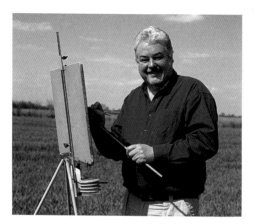

impressionistic style which makes his work much sought after. His expertise and technical knowledge about materials and equipment earned him the position of product adviser to the French companies Conté and Canson for many years.

Ian has produced many instructional videos during his long career, many of which accompany his television series. He is a winner of the Landscape Award at the Mall Galleries in London, an elected member of the British Watercolour Society and also a Fellow of the International Guild of Artists.

INTRODUCTION

To fully understand the methods of the Norwich
School, I have evolved a unique stage-by-stage
method which has helped hundreds of aspiring
watercolourists master the techniques of this style.
There is no such thing as the correct method, but
there are some basic simple rules that can help to
give you an understanding of
this very challenging medium,
thereby creating brilliantly
lit, evocative paintings
easily and cheerily. This
book contains all you
need to know to

Horsey Mill, Norfolk
29 x 41 cm (12 x 16 in)
Often walking around a
subject can give you a
better view as shown in
this study of Horsey Mill.

achieve this in your own painting. Watercolour painting has become a way of life to me. It has taken me to beautiful places and has always been stimulating, providing me with hours of pleasure and a career in fine art, teaching and television. You are about to become part of it. Welcome to the world of watercolour.

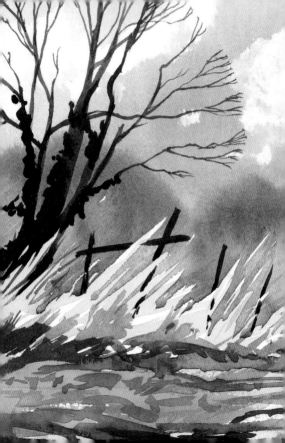

PART ONE

Getting started

Having decided that you want to paint in watercolour, what's your next step? For many of us, it's a visit to our local art shop, an Aladdin's cave where we will spend hours of our precious time and lots of hard-earned money. I suggest that you read the next chapter before you buy any art materials, but the best advice is always to keep them simple and get only what you need. You must also master a few basic watercolour techniques, which are explained in detail in the following pages. Then you will be ready to start painting.

Winter Furrows
23 x 23 cm (9 x 9 in)
The simplest subjects often make the best paintings. Using a soft wet in wet background technique with a more detailed foreground, this simple tree makes a lovely fresh study.

MATERIALS

In order to paint successfully, you need some essential items of equipment. The less equipment you start with, the easier the whole process will become. You will learn very quickly how to use your equipment and materials if you keep them simple. There is no point in buying a lot of expensive items that you may never use.

Below: If you set your palette out as shown here, it will keep your colours clean. Never put reds and blues next to your earth colours – keep them well apart.

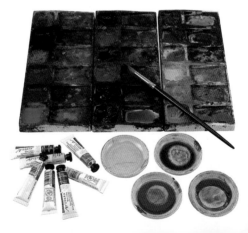

PAINTS

First of all, you will need some watercolour paints,
which have been specially developed by artists
working with manufacturers for over 200 years. Any
old paint will simply not work. The initial outlay on
basic materials needed will probably surprise you,
but you can't paint without the right equipment
any more than you can play golf with a cricket bat.

Initially, you will need only about eight colours.
Tube paints are the easiest to use and are cheaper
than solid colours, which are really designed for
painting outdoors. There are two basic types of
watercolour paint: Students' colours and Artists'
colours. The difference is that Students' colours are
bulked out with extenders whereas Artists' colours
are virtually all pigment.

The Students' range will cost you far less and virtually
every art shop will stock them. When you're starting
out, they are more than adequate. You will learn how
to mix colours together, and how to apply washes. The
colours you create with Students' colours will not be
as bright or as dark as Artists' colours, but while you're
learning this will not really matter. As you progress
and colours begin to run out, replace them with the
more expensive Artists' colours.

Which colours?

The initial outlay for a whole palette of paints would be enormous so buying one or two at a time makes sense. Earth colours (Raw Sienna, Yellow Ochre, Burnt Sienna and Burnt Umber) are better purchased in larger 14 ml tubes as you will use a lot of these. With other colours, such as Cadmium Yellow, a small 5 ml tube is sufficient. Paints often go hard in the tube before you ever get round to using them up, and they seem to last for years!

Beginner's palette

As a beginner, you will need some transparent colours and some opaque colours. The usual beginner's palette (see the illustration opposite) is the same as that of most landscape artists although they will add a few more colours. Your palette should always have some 'earth colours' as a base, together with some blues, which are mixed with the earth colours to make your greens. You don't need blacks or whites. In most boxes of colours, there is usually a Chinese White. You don't need it – hand it in at your local police station now! You might want to keep the black, even though you will hardly ever use it.

Some other colours you might like to add to this basic palette include the following: Coeruleum, Hooker's Green, Payne's Grey, Alizarin Crimson and Neutral Tint.

It is worth bearing in mind that the more colours you have on your palette, the more confusing the mixing will become. Mastering your mixing is the first real hurdle you need to cross in order to paint well.

BASIC COLOURS

Raw Sienna
transparent yellow

Yellow Ochre
opaque yellow

Cadmium Yellow
opaque, warm yellow

Burnt Sienna
transparent red

Burnt Umber
transparent brown

French Ultramarine
transparent, warm blue

Prussian Blue
transparent, intense blue

Cobalt Blue
transparent, cool blue

Above: As a beginner, you don't need to buy a lot of expensive paints. The eight colours shown here will be sufficient and can be mixed to create other colours.

BRUSHES

Unlike paints, your brush selection will be better if you invest in quality. There are thousands of brushes out there to buy. Just bear in mind that you only need about five, so it's worth spending that little bit more on them; they will do the job better and certainly last longer.

Natural hair has barbs on it and it is these barbs that hold the paint, so the more natural hair the better even though they are more expensive than man-made fibres. Nylon brushes have smooth fibres and therefore do not work so well.

However, most brush manufacturers now offer a range that are a mixture of natural hair and nylon fibres. These are less expensive than pure sable hair and, frankly, when you're starting out, they will do just as well. The exception is a large sky brush, which is usually made from squirrel hair.

Natural hair is a ready meal for moths, so you will need something in which to keep your brushes. I use a bamboo mat which protects their delicate tips and allows them to breathe. This is important; if you put your brushes away wet and sealed up, they will soon become mouldy and will be ruined.

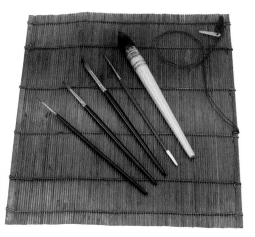

Above: A bamboo mat is ideal for keeping your brushes safe and protecting the tips. Always wash your brushes well after use and then allow them to dry thoroughly, tip upwards, before rolling them up in the mat. The brushes shown here are (from left to right): round brushes Nos. 2, 4 and 8, a rigger and a large squirrel mop brush.

OTHER EQUIPMENT

Other items you will need are some masking fluid, waterproof ink, watersoluble pencils, artists' sponges, masking tape, some tissue (for blotting), drawing pencils and plastic erasers. All these items are worth purchasing together with a standard drawing board.

After several weeks of painting, you may well feel that you need some more equipment. Many of these items, you can easily make yourself. For example, a mahlstick is extremely useful when you are painting, and you can make your own from a macramé bead and a short length of dowel.

Right: You will find these items of equipment useful: sketchbooks, pencils, masking tape, ink, an eraser, scalpel, rubber bands, drawing pins, a mahlstick and masking fluid.

TIP You may be surprised to discover that one of your most useful painting tools is a credit card. You can use one to etch out boulders and tree trunks (see page 31). For obvious reasons, it is best always to use an old card for this.

Art shops are very tempting, and there are always some items that it's better to buy than try to make yourself. If you're going to be painting outside, a metal easel, a lightweight drawing board and collapsible water pots will come in handy. You may also need some of the following items: large bulldog clips to stop the paper blowing away, plastic palettes, plastic knives and a fishing box to carry everything in.

PAPER

Choosing the right paper may confuse even the most experienced artist. As a beginner, you need a wood pulp paper, but it must be a watercolour paper. Many watercolour pads are unsuitable, so ask specifically for watercolour paper. The most common is Bockingford. This paper will do everything you expect of it, and it comes with either a not or a rough surface.

The weight of paper is actually its thickness. A good weight is 300 gsm or 140 lb. A less weighty paper than this is usually too thin to put a lot of water on and will cockle when paint is applied. Some of the heavier papers are difficult to use.

Paper surfaces

There are three basic watercolour paper surfaces from which you can choose, and these are as follows:

Hot pressed: This very smooth paper is good for working with ink and pen, but not for broken washes.

Not (or cold pressed): The surface of this paper is impressed, using a felt blanket. It's a much better choice for painting subjects such as architecture and boats where you will need to create straight edges. Indeed, it is the ideal surface for beginners.

NOT PAPER

Simple line from the brush tip

Broken lines from the brush edge

Pushing the paint along the paper

Using a large soft brush

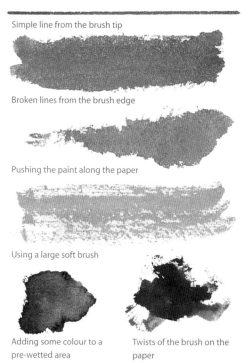

Adding some colour to a
pre-wetted area

Twists of the brush on the
paper

Rough: This paper surface is impressed with a woollen blanket, and is usually the same on both sides; thus both sides can be used. This is great for landscapes and broken brushwork.

Different papers

When you have mastered the basic techniques, you may wish to experiment with some different papers. Changing the paper will always alter the appearance of your work. You will find that while some papers suit your style, others won't. Wood pulp papers are the simplest ones to use, basically because you can easily lift out any part you like. With a cotton paper, you cannot lift out, although the paints will always look brighter, and wet in wet techniques will be more effective because cotton absorbs water better.

> **TIP:** You won't need to stretch the paper; simply cut it to size and attach it to a board with a piece of masking tape at each corner. Stretching paper is a poor use of your valuable painting time and can ruin many papers. Personally, I always paint on 140 lb weight paper and never stretch it first, as it expands when water is applied. I simply keep pulling it tight at each corner; it never fails me.

ROUGH PAPER

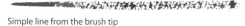

Simple line from the brush tip

Broken lines from the brush edge

Pushing the paint along the paper

Using a large soft brush

Adding some colour to a
pre-wetted area

Twists of the brush on the
paper

TECHNIQUES

To paint well you must control your water, colour and brushwork. Colour is your alphabet and brushwork your language. You need to learn to judge how much colour, how much water and which brush to use.

MIXING A BASIC WASH

When you start mixing washes, always use a clean area of your palette. With a No. 8 round brush, add some clean water, about a teaspoonful, to your palette. Then dip your No. 4 round brush into French Ultramarine until about half of the brush is covered in paint. Add this to the water in the palette and mix well together. You have now made your first simple wash, which is the basis of all watercolour. Never put the paint in first; this will simply waste paint and make the water dirty.

Using your No. 8 brush, paint a small area of the paper. Try to get this even without overbrushing it too much. Overbrushing will make your colours look dirty by disturbing the surface of the paper. Add a similar amount of water again, mix well and paint a new area. When this dries, you will see that the first is darker than the second. This is why we do not use white to make colours lighter;

we simply add more water to them to make the wash paler. It is difficult to judge just how dark the wash needs to be, especially when any blues have been added as they always dry lighter than they appear when wet.

The first two colours shown below have a dimpled pattern – granulation. It occurs when the pigment, a mineral, settles into the hollows in the paper. Use this technique to create interest in washes. When you don't want granulation, simply tilt your board to a more vertical angle and the wash will dry smooth.

1 With a No. 8 brush, first paint a wash of French Ultramarine.

2 Add more water to it. Let them dry flat and see how much lighter the second wash is.

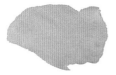

3 Add even more water, tilt the board and leave to dry. It will dry smooth with no granulation.

MIXING A TWO-COLOUR WASH

Try the basic wash from the previous page again, but this time using Raw Sienna (see below). You will see that blues change more than the earth colours. Try mixing French Ultramarine with Raw Sienna (see opposite), and then paint another area. Do the same again with French Ultramarine and Yellow Ochre. The mix with Yellow Ochre will appear more solid than the mix with the Sienna. This is because the Sienna is transparent and the Ochre is opaque.

This is one of the most important washes to work at. If there is no difference between these washes when they dry, then you are adding either too much or not enough water. The wash should not be thick; on the contrary, it should be very wet. The two greens shown opposite (top) are the most important ones you will ever use. They are the basic landscape greens.

1 Paint a basic wash of Raw Sienna.

2 Now add some water and watch it dry.

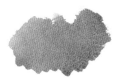

1 Paint a transparent wash of Raw Sienna and French Ultramarine.

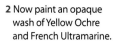

2 Now paint an opaque wash of Yellow Ochre and French Ultramarine.

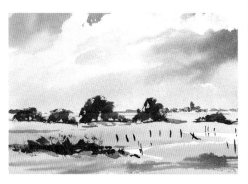

East Anglian Landscape
12 x 23 cm (5 x 9 in)
In this simple landscape, the distant background greens are Raw Sienna based (transparent) whereas the foreground greens are Yellow Ochre based (opaque).

WET AND DAMP WASHES

Having got the hang of mixing washes of the same strengths, you can now move on to using wet washes with damp washes. This useful technique is needed for creating subtle changes in colour. However, you should always remember the following guidelines.

• A brush loaded with water makes a wet wash.
• A brush with the excess water shaken out of it makes a damp wash.

Make a wash and paint a small area, and then paint a different coloured wash next to it. This is one of the many mixing techniques that make watercolours so fascinating. You never know what will happen.

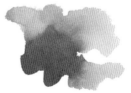

1 First of all, paint an area of Burnt Sienna.

2 Next to the Burnt Sienna, paint a damp wash of Prussian Blue. Leave the board flat and see how the colours run and mix together.

RESERVOIR TECHNIQUE

This technique produces subtle changes in the same colour; it's great for painting roofs, walls and solid areas in order to create extra interest in your paintings.

A fairly strong colour wash is washed onto the paper and then teased around using a damp brush. This will create varied depths and strengths. See how some of the wash dries lighter where more water is added. Practise this as much as you like; mastering this technique will greatly enhance any watercolour you paint. Next try a very wet wash with a drier wash added as shown below.

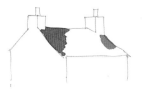

1 The colour is washed on quite strongly in a couple of small areas, usually to show edges or corners.

2 Whilst still wet, the colour is washed out and spread using a brush with clean water. The effect created will give you a random depth of colour, ideal for walls and roofs.

ETCHING

Use the pointed handle of your brush for etching wet paint. Creating lines from the original colour looks better than drawing them in later with a pencil or pen.

Above: For planking on boats and timber buildings, paint the base colour and then etch in the lines with a brush handle.

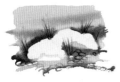

Left: A little dark brown was added whilst still wet so it ran into the Raw Sienna. Grasses and pebbles were etched in with a brush handle.

DRY BRUSH TECHNIQUE

A foreground can look good with a broken wash laid over a solid area of colour.

Right: Using a nearly dry mop brush, paint the strokes in one direction only or the gaps begin to fill in.

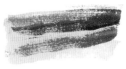

CREDIT CARD TECHNIQUE

This is not a new technique; the early watercolourists used a specially trimmed thumb nail or a thin piece of ivory instead of a credit card. The wet paint is simply removed with the edge of the card to leave areas of white paper. The results are visually more exciting than those achieved with masking techniques.

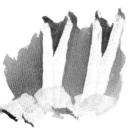

1 Wash in a large area of colour as a background. Quickly scrape out white areas before the paint dries, using the card like a window cleaner uses his squeegee. This works best on wood pulp paper.

2 When the first wash is dry, add the details. Turn the tree shapes into Silver Birch, using Burnt Sienna and Burnt Umber with a rigger for the bark. A few grasses are added using a rigger.

LIFTING OUT

Lifting out paint with some tissue and a sponge will create a different effect to using a credit card, but only works well on wood pulp based papers, the most commonly available being Bockingford.

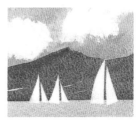

Right: The sky and water were painted with French Ultramarine and the clouds blotted out with a tissue whilst wet. When dry, mountains were added with Raw Sienna and French Ultramarine and left to dry. A stencil of sail shapes was cut out of paper and, using a damp sponge, the sails were lifted out.

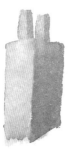

Left: A solid area of colour can be shaped by blotting part of it with a wet sponge to lighten the colour. I masked this chimney stack with tape, sponged out until the area was light enough, then removed the tape and, hey presto, a three-dimensional chimney stack appeared. Be careful removing the tape or it will pull the paper up.

MASKING FLUID TECHNIQUE

With masking fluid you can paint freely but keep details, either by leaving some white paper or retaining colour. Mask the details with fluid, applying it with an old brush.

1 The reeds were painted as a solid area; when dry, they were put in with masking fluid.

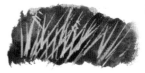

2 When a dark wash was added, the masked areas resisted the paint and appeared light.

CANDLE WAX TECHNIQUE

Wax works in the same way, but it is more random and can't be removed. Use it for creating ripples in water. Don't overdo it as it cannot be painted over.

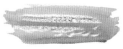

Right: The wax can be drawn on in straight lines or added as scallops for running water. Add the paint on top.

BRUSHWORK

Every brush will create a different mark, and how you hold it will change the strokes. Brushwork is the language of all painters – the paper and colours are only the mediums we use. The marks we make determine our personal style of painting. The brush strokes below were painted with the tip, holding the brush conventionally. See how different brushes make lines of varying thicknesses.

No. 2 nylon pointed rigger

No. 2 round pointed brush (50% nylon)

No. 4 round pointed brush (50% nylon)

No. 8 round pointed brush (50% nylon)

No. 4 large squirrel hair mop brush

Using the brush on its side

Doing this, you get different marks. The rigger is not included as only the tip can be used. With smaller round brushes, you get rougher edges. Larger brushes hold more paint so the marks are longer before breaking up.

No. 2 round pointed brush (50% nylon)

No. 4 round pointed brush (50% nylon)

No. 8 round pointed brush (50% nylon)

No. 4 large squirrel hair mop brush

Using a rigger

Use a rigger when painting delicate areas, such as twigs on winter trees.

MIXING COLOURS

Having mastered mixing washes and the art of brushwork,
your next challenge is colour mixing. Making a simple
colour chart will help you to learn your colours – and
remember which ones you need. This takes a couple of
hours but is time well spent. Until you know your colours,
any painting you try to do will be at best a lucky accident.

The colour chart illustrated opposite is created by
mixing equal amounts of the colours on the chart.
By adding your original colour palette to the chart,
you will quickly recognize any colour.

1 Start with Raw Sienna and paint the first square on
   the top line.

2 Now mix a little French Ultramarine and paint the
   first square on the second line to the left.

3 Mix these two together and then paint the second
   square from the left on the second line.

4 Clean up, then add a square of Prussian Blue to the
   third line down.

5 Mix with the Raw Sienna to create the next square
   in, and so on.

Cleaning up each time will probably seem a bit wasteful but you need this chart to have clean colours if it is to be any good later. When you have completed the chart, you will see that the colours made with the Siennas are lighter looking than those made with either the Ochre or the Umber. This is because the Siennas are transparent colours. You will also now have a complete guide to the range of greens that can be made from the Earth Palette.

Below: It's amazing how many colours can be created from just a few. Cover this chart in plastic to make it a permanent aid. It will become your best friend.

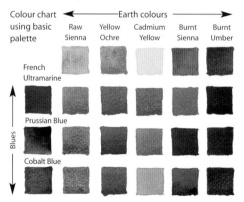

Colour chart using basic palette — Earth colours →

	Raw Sienna	Yellow Ochre	Cadmium Yellow	Burnt Sienna	Burnt Umber
French Ultramarine					
Prussian Blue					
Cobalt Blue					

Blues

TRY A LITTLE EXERCISE

By now you should feel that you are ready to paint, so here is an easy little exercise which will help you to put it all together and get you going. Use the picture below as your guide. Decide how large a piece of paper you will need for your painting. Controlling your brushwork and washes will be easier if you think small. I usually suggest something a touch larger than a postcard.

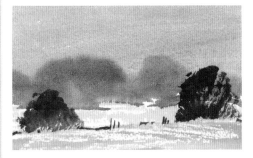

Simple Landscape
12 x 22 cm (5 x 9 in)
You can use your earth colours and blues to create a simple little landscape. You could try using the same technique to create several of these natural scenes. Experiment with varying the trees and maybe adding a barn but keep them small.

1 Tape the paper down on your drawing board with a few strips of masking tape.

2 Mix a wash of pale French Ultramarine, using a large No. 8 brush and then paint this wash over the top two-thirds of the paper.

3 Whilst this is still wet, paint a little Burnt Umber into it, using a No. 4 brush. Hold the drawing board up vertically and let the paint dry.

4 Using the edge of a No. 8 brush, add a stripe of Raw Sienna across the painting underneath the blue and the Burnt Umber. Allow to dry.

5 When this is completely dry, add a wash of Yellow Ochre underneath.

6 Finally, mix a wash of Yellow Ochre with French Ultramarine and, using the edge of a No. 4 brush, blob in a few trees.

Congratulations! You have just painted your first landscape. In the following chapters, we will look in much greater detail at how to plan your paintings, using my simple seven-stage step-by-step system (see page 58), and thereby add dimension and distance to them.

SKETCHING AND PLANNING

A sketchbook has always been the life blood of all painters. Keeping one not only helps you to record what you see but it also helps you to learn to observe. Draw whenever you can – anything at all, it does not have to be grand. Don't feel embarrassed by your drawings – they're for your eyes only and you don't have to show them to anyone!

TIP To avoid running out of paper, with a pencil, draw a small rectangular page in the centre of your sketchbook page. Sketch in this initially and when your sketch grows out of your box, you can let it grow in any direction.

SKETCHING EQUIPMENT

Try to vary your sketches by using pens as well as pencils. With good-quality paper you can even incorporate a little colour. Record anything and everything. You will soon have a collection of sketches that you can feel proud of, and these can become the basis for many paintings with the use of your local photocopy shop!

It may seem wasteful but draw on only one side of the pages in your sketchbook; otherwise any pencil sketches will be transferred with pressure over the preceding pages and your work will get ruined. However, if all your sketches are in ink, this will not be a problem.

Pens and pencils

For drawing, use a 3B pencil which will make fine lines or dark areas easily. However, keep it sharp. There are many pens to choose from. I usually use a 0.5 mm tip pen with watersoluble ink. This can be washed over with water to create greys and tone.

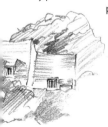

Left: This subject is all about the angles and lines of the roofs. You can show their texture far better with a pencil than with pen and ink.

ENLARGING SKETCHES

Lots of different ideas are circulated about making
sketches larger and how best to transfer them to
watercolour paper, using grids and a variety of other
methods. All I can say is that the advent of a photocopy
shop in virtually every high street has made it so easy.
Your sketch can be enlarged to any size you like, and it
need not be taken out of your sketchbook. Then, by
fixing it to a window at home with masking tape,
placing some watercolour paper over it and taping it
down, you can trace it straight through. Although
watercolour paper looks opaque, it isn't. You can see
straight through it, unless you are wearing something
light which reflects light back from you.

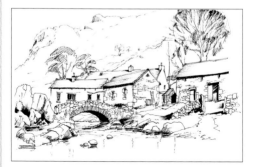

The same applies when you are working outside. Use the car windows, especially a tailgate. It's great when you've made a drawing but the painting has failed. If this happens, you can draw it all again in minutes.

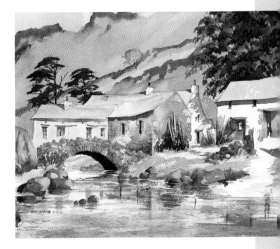

Watendlath, Cumbria
38 x 56 cm (15 x 22 in)
This was painted in the studio from the sketch (left). Simply by having been there and making the sketch I had a feel for the subject even months later.

PERSPECTIVE

In any painting or sketch, the perspective will alter according to your eye level. The viewpoint is the position from which you look at a scene, whether it's a landscape or a building. Thus, the perspective will change depending on your position and whether you are higher or lower than what you are looking at. The nearer objects are to you, the larger they will be; the further away they are, the smaller they become. The vanishing point is where the perspective lines meet.

Right: Your viewpoint will always be at eye level and the position in which you are sitting.

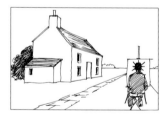

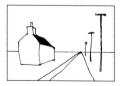

Left: In this normal view, on level ground, the horizon is at the viewer's eye level, halfway up the building.

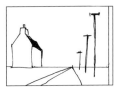

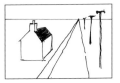

Left: When looking up at the house, the eye level and vanishing point on the horizon are at floor height.

Right: When looking down on the house, the vanishing point and eye level are much higher.

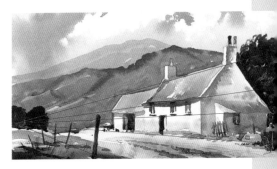

Moorland Farm
28 x 38 cm (11 x 15 in)
In this simple painting of a moorland farm, the perspective lines all converge at the vanishing point.

Fixed point perspective

All you need for this is a sharp pencil, a drawing pin and some elastic bands tied together.

1 At eye level, draw a line faintly across the painting and mark the spot in front of you.

2 Draw in the end of the first building. Put a pin in the spot in front of you and, with the elastic bands tied together, mark in the lines of the gutter, roof and base. The windows and doors can be shown by first drawing the front upright.

3 Using the elastic bands, draw in the tops and bottoms. All the vertical lines stay vertical.

4 Now that the first building is in perspective, do the same for the remaining buildings, including those on the other side of the street.

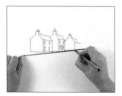

Left: After constructing the basic guidelines, simply by drawing in the facing wall of each building, the elastic band will do the rest of the work for you.

Going round the bend

Fixed point perspective works well for a straight street. However, if the street has a bend in it, don't worry – just do the following and your perspective will always work.

1 Simply move the drawing pin along your line an inch or so for each building. You will soon see that the row of buildings then appears to go 'round the bend'.

2 On the sketch below you can see how the drawing pin has been moved by the stars that I have added to the paper to mark each spot. You can make your buildings go from left or right, up or down, by using the same method. It could not be simpler.

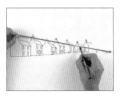

Left: Where you need to go round the bend, simply move the pin to left or right for each building. The more the pin is moved, the greater the effect of the turn.

TIP The holes that you make in the paper will almost disappear after it has been wetted. Perspective was never easier than this!

WORKING FROM PHOTOGRAPHS

If you need to work from photographs, then always make a sketch first. You can enlarge this (see page 42) and then transfer it to your watercolour paper. Not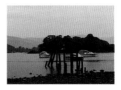

only will it enable you to find your focal plane more easily (see page 56) but it will also ensure that your

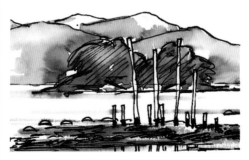

Above: A simple line drawing helps you understand the elements of the painting and where your background, foreground and middle distance are. It takes only a few minutes to do and can save you hours!

watercolour is a real painting and not just a copy of a picture. You can still think about it as your original. The worst thing that anyone can say about your paintings, however well-meaning, is that 'they are just like photographs'; then you know that you have failed gloriously.

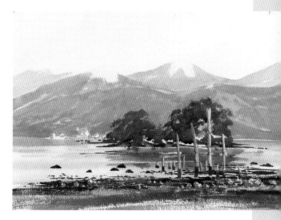

The Buttertubs, Derwent Water, Cumbria
38 x 56 cm (15 x 22 in)
This painting has a very light background, a dark middle ground and a strong foreground with the posts left light against the dark trees.

LEARNING TO LOOK

When you are outside looking at a view, your angle of vision is probably nearly 100 degrees. There will be so much potential subject matter that you won't know where to start. However, look closely at the subject. What attracted you to it? Try to determine this first as it will help you to plan out your painting. Many beginners complain that they don't know what to paint, but there is a subject everywhere, and your problem is deciding what to put in and what to leave out.

Right: I used an ink pen, adding texture to show the detail in the foreground. I kept the backgound simple and light. Dark areas were added with a brush pen.

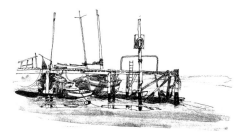

Above: These boats against a jetty require an accurate sketch. A waterproof ink pen is ideal for this type of fine line work.

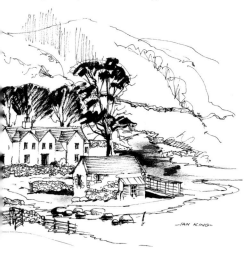

PLANNING YOUR PAINTING

When planning a painting, always start with your 'subject'. Have a look round. Is there anything in the background that would look good behind the subject such as a few trees or a distant hill? They don't have to be there for you to put them in. Borrow them and do the same for the foreground.

You may wish to leave out anything modern if you want your painting to look timeless. Cars and telephone boxes may be there but seldom add anything to your sketches or watercolours. Once you have planned the background, subject and foreground, make a sketch. You may need to write down a few ideas and notes about colours, the date and time of day. You could also take a photograph for future reference.

When composing a painting, the classic 'rule of thirds' helps you achieve the right balance as well as making it look more dynamic.

- Don't place the subject right in the middle; this will look boring.

- Position it a third of the way in or a third of the way up – somewhere slightly off centre.

- Place buildings, mountains, the horizon, trees or foreground posts either a third of the way in from left or right, or from the bottom or top.

The example overleaf shows how the rule of thirds can be used to maximize a painting.

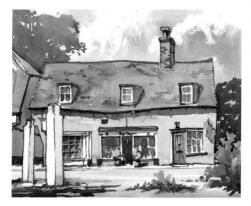

Haywain Tearoom, Flatford
28 x 38 cm (11 x 15 in)
The tearoom seems central but the background and the foreground have been altered to make the thirds rule work.

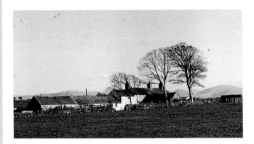

Above: In this photograph of an Anglesey farm, the mountains of Snowdonia are in the distance.

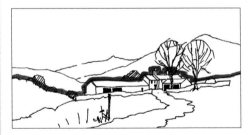

Above: In my sketch, I have enlarged the mountains and moved the farm to the right so that the trees are one third of the way in from the right. The red line shows the focal plane (see page 56).

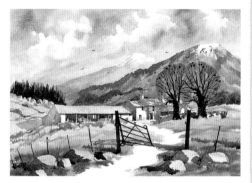

Farm at Pentraeth, Anglesey
38 x 40 cm (15 x 16 in)
In the finished picture, a foreground has been created from a
plain field by adding a path to lead the eye into the painting.
A post or two has added extra dimension. This demonstrates
effectively how using the rule of thirds can maximize the
impact of a painting.

TIP As artists, we've all got a JCB in our back pockets.
Unlike photographers, we can move or demolish anything.
Your judgement will improve with time but, as a general
rule, if a building, tree or object isn't going to do any work
in your sketch, then leave it out.

THE FOCAL PLANE

When you are planning your paintings, do a quick sketch to help you find the focal plane. You can divide your painting into three planes:

1 The background, or furthest plane.

2 The middle distance, which is closer to you.

3 The foreground, which is nearest to you.

Your subject will nearly always be placed in the middle distance. Behind is the background where objects will diminish in size and will be painted transparently. In front is the foreground, where any objects will be larger as they are closer to you, and this is usually painted opaquely.

A horizontal line drawn across your painting over your subject is referred to as the focal plane. This is the dividing line between the background and foreground and anything above it will be furthest away from you and therefore smaller and more transparent.

This is the key to painting successfully in the style of the Norwich School. The focal plane determines where your sky is painted down to and where you will use Raw Sienna or Yellow Ochre in mixing your colours.

Everything works around the focal plane in your painting so it is worth taking a little time to be sure that you understand how to find it.

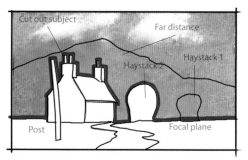

Above: Everything behind the focal plane, except clouds, will have a blue wash painted over it to help it recede. Haystack 1 is washed with blue but haystack 2 (in front of the focal plane) is left white as is the subject and any light areas in the foreground.

Right: The foreground and background create balance and depth. Paint backgrounds transparently, usually over the sky wash, and foregrounds opaquely. The focal plane is where the transparency begins.

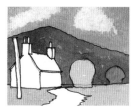

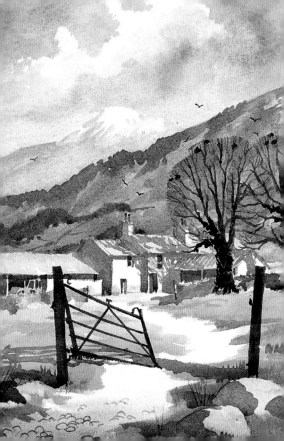

PART TWO

The seven stages

To paint successfully, first you need to understand the subject. My seven-stage system will help you master the different processes. We start with an overview of a typical landscape and then break it down into seven stages in step-by-step detail. We then take a broader view of each stage. This not only makes the process easier but also takes the terror out of it, helping you to focus on your subject, colour and technique.

Farm at Pentraeth, Anglesey
40 x 38 cm (16 x 15 in)
There is a subject everywhere, even though you may need to re-structure it to make it work better. This painting is a classic example of what can be achieved with a simple subject.

THE BASIC STAGES

Here is an overview of the seven stages of landscape painting. Each stage is examined in detail in the following pages as I show you, step by step, how to build up your painting.

Raw
Sienna

Yellow
Ochre

Naples
Yellow

Burnt
Sienna

Burnt
Umber

Alizarin
Crimson

French
Ultramarine

Prussian
Blue

Cobalt
Blue

Coeruleum

STAGE 1:
The sky

Bringing the sky down to the focal plane gives everything in the background a blue base, making it recede. The clouds and snowy peaks are blotted out with some tissue before adding the darker elements in the sky.

STAGE 2: The background

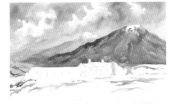

Layers of transparent hills are painted over the blue base to create depth. The more detailed mountain has stronger colours added to imply rocky outcrops. These colours are also added to the foreground for the light and dark bands.

STAGE 3: The foreground

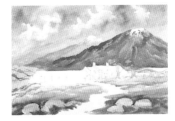

Transparent washes are added, first with an opaque wash in the foreground. Details are added, using a credit card and also by etching with a brush handle, before the dark greens are added wet in wet.

STAGE 4: The main subject

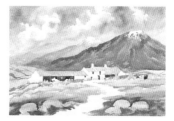

Many beginners start with the subject but this makes painting the background difficult. By painting the subject at this stage, it will not be necessary to add as much detail as we may have thought – less is often better. Simple darks added at this stage begin to describe the entire subject.

STAGE 5: The trees

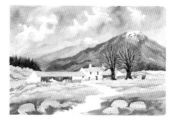

These are better painted before the details are added. A lot of the detail we might have thought about including then becomes unnecessary. Trees increase the sense of depth in our paintings, and positioning them is important.

STAGE 6: The details

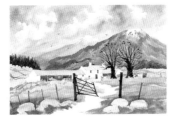

'If in doubt, leave it out.' When adding details, it is important that each one adds something to the painting. If it doesn't, it is best to leave it out. A great many paintings are ruined at this stage by over embellishment.

STAGE 7: The shadows

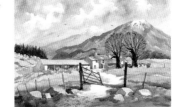

This is the final stage where the action takes place. Until the shadows go in, the watercolour will look quite flat and unlit. However, shadows can transform a study, making it sunny and three-dimensional.

STAGE 1: THE SKY

Before starting to paint, fix your chosen size of paper to your board (as described on page 22). You will not manage a subject like this well if you cannot turn your paper round. Also, get ready everything that you will need, including paints, brushes, palette and some tissue for blotting. Lastly, make sure that your brushes are clean.

PLANNING STAGE

Enhance the background and create a foreground path to lead the eye into the painting. Determine your focal plane (shown by the

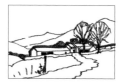

red line). Behind it will be transparent colour; in front, it'll be mostly opaque. This shows where the sky wash will stop.

STAGE 1

Mix a wash of Cobalt Blue and another of French Ultramarine. Turn the painting upside down; it is easier to paint a sky from this angle. Wet the sky area from the focal plane to the top, carefully taking the edge over the buildings. Paint the entire sky with Cobalt Blue, using a large mop.

STAGE 2

Turn your painting the right way up to see the shapes of the clouds. Blot out cloud and snow shapes with tissue to get dry and wet areas in the

sky. Into the top wet areas, add French Ultramarine, using a No. 8 brush, and work the blue in to the sky.

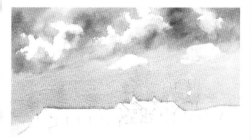

STAGE 3

Add shadows to the underside of the clouds with a mixture of Burnt Umber and French Ultramarine. Use a No. 8 brush. Wash the colour along the underside and left-hand sides of the clouds, teasing it up into the centre. Blot the middle area light again with some tissue if this should go wrong.

STAGE 2: THE BACKGROUND

Good painting is all about planning, and it is well
worth taking the time to plan each stage of your
painting. Before creating the background, think
about what you want it to look like. The mountains
will look exactly as you make them, and there are
four separate stages involved in creating them.

STAGE 1

Build up the mountain
colour layer upon layer. Mix
French Ultramarine and Raw
Sienna and wash in the
mountain shapes, leaving

the snow unpainted. Lightly swipe out the misty effect
between the two last mountains with tissue. Dry, then add
a little of the same colour to the two large tree trunks.

STAGE 2

Add more colour to your
wash, then paint in the two
nearest mountains, making
your brushwork 'go with the
flow' of the landscape to

give it form. Leave the snow as white paper. Wipe in another
misty layer between these two mountains.

STAGE 3

Mix more French Ultramarine into your wash and paint the nearest mountain and a little of the foreground to create dark and light bands across it.

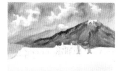

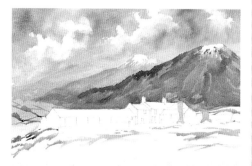

STAGE 4

Add more French Ultramarine and some Burnt Umber to the wash and paint in the rocks and gullies on the nearest mountain. Tilt your board upside down and let the paint run up against the sky to create rock effects. Begin painting the hedges and walls in the middle distance behind the farm. Do this very simply. You will not see any birds in the trees at that distance so don't be tempted to put some in.

STAGE 3: THE FOREGROUND

The techniques used in the foreground of a painting, when perfected, will allow you to create many different but lively effects. However, to be effective, you need to practise them so before painting the foreground try them out on the back of an old painting. Watercolour paper is always double sided so you can do this anytime.

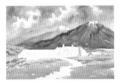

STAGE 1

Wash the entire middle distance with some Raw Sienna, behind and in front of the farm buildings, leaving the path white.

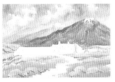

STAGE 2

Mix a wash of Yellow Ochre, then a strong wash of Burnt Sienna with Prussian Blue – this will make a deep green to use as wet in wet for the

foreground. Mix it before you start painting; otherwise it will be too dry for the second wash to work. Have your credit card ready. Paint the foreground with the Yellow Ochre and then create the boulders using your card.

STAGE 3

Wash in the dark green (Burnt Sienna and Prussian Blue), using a large brush. Tilt your board to help this run down into the painting.

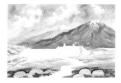

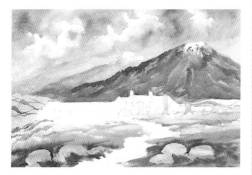

STAGE 4

Before Stage 3 dries, etch in the grasses and pebbles with your brush handle. The paint needs to be wet. If it doesn't work, it will be because it has dried.

STAGE 4: THE MAIN SUBJECT

Although, at first glance, the architecture appears
quite detailed, look again and you will see that
actually it is painted very simply. The illusion of detail
is one of the best tricks to learn in watercolour.
Nothing looks worse than an over-painted subject.

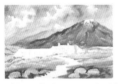

STAGE 1

Buildings often look as if
they are floating about and
not part of the painting. To
ground them, just paint a
dirty wash along the base
of the walls, having washed the walls first in clean water.
Mix the green from the foreground with Burnt Umber to
create the right colour. Add to the base of the walls. It will
begin to creep up into the wet area so tilt your board
upright to stop it flowing too far.

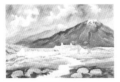

STAGE 2

Paint in the green lichen on
the roofs using Raw Sienna
and Cobalt Blue, following
the slope of the tiles. Leave
some odd bits of white.

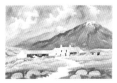

STAGE 3

It's time to add a few darks but don't be tempted to use black. Instead, mix a wash of Burnt Umber and French Ultramarine and paint the walls, holding the brush sideways to get a broken effect. Paint the darks in the doors, windows and inside the open barn. Leave the latter abstract.

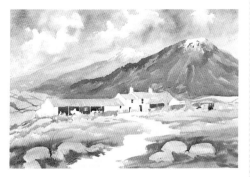

STAGE 4

The roof slates can now be painted over the lichen. Do this with pale Cobalt Blue. Be sure the brush strokes come down with the angle of the roofs. You can now see the effect of the whites that you left – great for a roof, aren't they?

STAGE 5: THE TREES

Most paintings can be dramatically improved by the careful placing of trees. You don't have to put them in where they really are – you have artistic licence. Put them where they will do some work or leave them out totally. Remember the JCB!

STAGE 1

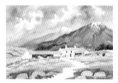

Brush in the distant trees at the foot of the mountains very simply with a wash of Raw Sienna, Burnt Umber and French Ultramarine. However, don't paint them too dark. They break up the distance and create extra depth in your painting.

STAGE 2

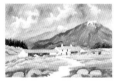

The distant conifers are a classic example of trees that work. They weren't in the real landscape but they separate the background from the middle ground. With a wash of Burnt Umber and Prussian Blue, paint a spiky top and ragged bottom which will eventually look like rocks. Fill in the middle area. Dry, then paint on more spikes and a few areas of extra darks, keeping them fairly simple.

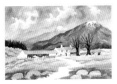

STAGE 3

The tall elm trees by the farm are painted with a mix of Burnt Umber and Prussian Blue. Draw a pencil edge for your winter trees. When the painting is dry, it will erase completely. Paint in the main trunks and branches, leaving the bases spiky to look like grass growing up in front.

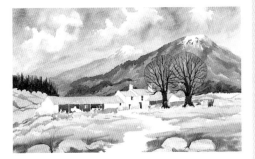

STAGE 4

Paint the branches and twigs with the same colour as in Stage 3 but thinned with a little water. Use a rigger for this (see page 135). Left-handed people may find it easier if they turn the painting upside down. Try to keep the lines quite thin – this takes a bit of practice!

STAGE 6: THE DETAILS

Many paintings are ruined by the fact that there is too much detail. Remember that you get the maximum effect with the minimum effort so resist the temptation to put everything in when you are painting the details. Often, creating the impression of something is more effective than showing it as it really is.

STAGE 1

Paint some ivy on the large trees. If any part of the tree looks wrong, then remedy the situation by covering it in ivy. Mix Burnt Umber with

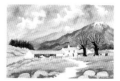

a touch of Prussian Blue for this. Use a No. 4 brush and paint the ivy with small, stabbing actions. Before it dries, push your brush handle into it to create the light growth lines.

STAGE 2

Wash the grass across the foreground of the painting, leaving the path white. Use a thin wash of Cadmium Yellow and Cobalt Blue.

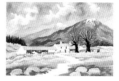

STAGE 3

Add the chimney pots with
Yellow Ochre and some dark
for the soot. Paint the door
and barn interior with Burnt
Sienna. Use Burnt Umber

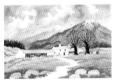

with French Ultramarine for the rooks' nests and birds. Use a
paler wash for the larger trees, keeping inside the pencil lines.

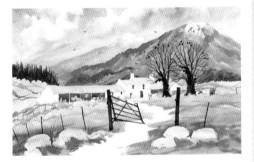

STAGE 4

Paint the posts and gate with a mix of French Ultramarine
and Burnt Umber. Leave the gate open to lead the viewer in
to the painting. If you can't paint a gate at an angle, leave it
out. Make the gate tall enough to break through the farm
and thereby create distance in your painting. Now add one or
two paler and thinner posts in the distance.

STAGE 7: THE SHADOWS

This stage of any painting is where the magic occurs. Your subject will suddenly appear three-dimensional and sunlit. Study the painting carefully before adding the shadows. If you go back to your original drawing and shade this in pencil before you paint, you'll know which direction the light is coming from and where the shadows need to be.

STAGE 1

Gradually add some French Ultramarine to plenty of Burnt Sienna until you get a grey. Test the colour on a scrap of paper. Let it dry,

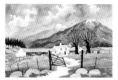

then hold it against your painting. If it's too dark, add more water to tone it down. Using a No. 6 brush with a good point, shade the rocks in front of the pine trees and the shadows of the farm on the ground. Then shade the farm buildings.

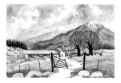

STAGE 2

When dry, use the same wash to shade the shadows from the trees across the ground and up over the roofs of the buildings. Add shadows on the stone walls.

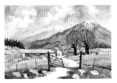

STAGE 3

Stir the wash again and then use to shade the shadows of the posts and gate. Add the shadows under the boulders and on the ground below them. Leave it all to dry thoroughly before moving on to the last stage and adding the finishing touches.

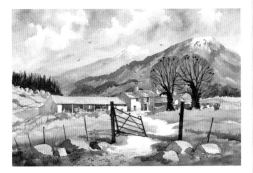

STAGE 4

Mix all the colours left on your palette, adding a touch more French Ultramarine. Wash the foreground with water, then add the wash across the front of the painting. Etch more pebbles across the path with a brush handle, then tilt the painting upright so the wash settles at the base. Leave it like this until dry.

PAINTING SKIES

Because skies are constantly changing, they never look the same. So many factors can affect them: the season, weather conditions, time of day. Skies may appear complicated but they are easy to paint.

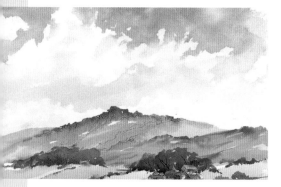

Simon's Seat, Wharfedale, Yorkshire
27 x 46 cm (10 x 18 in)
In this sky, there are three blues: Coeruleum for the initial wash; Cobalt Blue and French Ultramarine for the stronger wash. Burnt Umber was added to create the thundery tops to the clouds, and Raw Sienna finally for warmth.

BASIC TECHNIQUES

Master the basic technique of using graduated washes, then progress to creating various types of clouds.

Graduated wash

All you need is a graduated wash progressing from deep blue at the top to a pale blue at the horizon.

Left: Wet the whole area, then add a strong wash of French Ultramarine across the top with a mop. Keep brushing with horizontal strokes until you reach the bottom. Use watercolour paper for this.

Lifting out

The next step is to try lifting out lights for the clouds. For this, you will need some tissue.

Right: Wet the entire sky area to release the gelatine, or the colour will be absorbed straight into the paper and will not lift off effectively. Roll crumpled tissue across the sky to create the clouds.

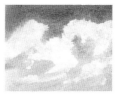

Wispy clouds

Are there any simple shapes you can see that will give you a lead as to how much white there is in a sky? Check this and then create some wispy clouds.

Left: To create wispy clouds, such as cirrus formations, fold some tissue to form a thin pad and then swipe it across your freshly painted wet sky at a slight angle.

Darker areas

To create darker areas, mix your blues together. Have plenty ready or you may get watermarks where the wet paint meets the drying paint.

Right: Paint the sky, lifting out the clouds, and, with a No. 4 brush, push darker paint into the wet areas, scrubbing it in to make it stay where you place it.

SHADOWS IN CLOUDS

To help define clouds , you can shade them like the subject on the ground. Add neutral tint to the sky blues to create a grey shadow tone, or mix the blues with Payne's Grey.

Right: Here, the sun is coming from the left so the shadows go along the base, up the right-hand sides of the clouds and are softened in the middle. The shadow tone is Light Red and French Ultramarine.

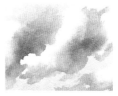

Peter Scott's Lighthouse, Lincolnshire
38 x 56 cm (15 x 22 in)
This was painted on a hot, sunny day. I washed a little of the shadow tone over the horizon to make it seem miles away.

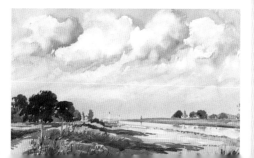

CREATING MOOD

The skies so far have all been tackled in one go.
However, more atmospheric effects can be created
when a sky is partially painted and then left to dry
before further layers of colour are added later. To
create subtle mood in your watercolour paintings, the
sky will usually need only a pale wash, often with a

Below: This working study is relatively small but it does show
how a simple subject can be changed by varying the sky and
the depth of colour in the background and foreground.

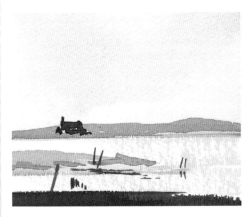

base wash of Raw Sienna to add a sense of warmth and depth; the subtlety is added to this afterwards as shown in the examples below.

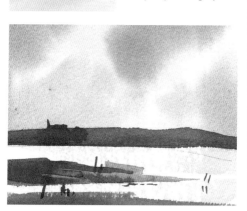

Left: I painted a simple cirrus sky. When the blues had dried , I washed them over with Raw Sienna for a hazy early morning sky.

Above: I have added Raw Sienna to the subject opposite. This creates a totally different, warming effect. Practise this with different subjects, adding a variety of skies.

MORNING AND EVENING SKIES

Adding a wash of Raw Sienna can create a warming effect which is useful when painting early morning or evening skies. After the initial wash of Raw Sienna, try adding a blue wash and graduate it down thinly.

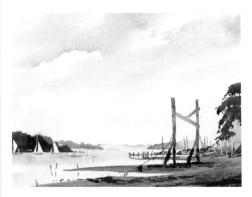

Early Morning on the Orwell, Suffolk
29 x 41 cm (11 x 16 in)
The painting was washed with Raw Sienna, then Cobalt Blue was washed in thinly to dry to nothing at the horizon. I added bands of stronger Cobalt Blue and lifted out the light gaps. Distance was created with transparent washes in the distance and opaque washes in the foreground.

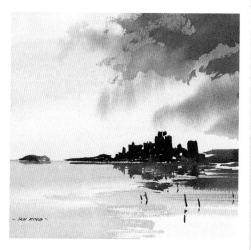

Evening Sky at Bamburgh Castle, Northumberland
22 x 32 cm (9 x 12 in)
Raw Sienna is the base, even under the sea wash. The pale sky
blue wash was added to the Sienna when dry and this was
strengthened for the sea. The remaining washes were made
from Light Red and a touch of Burnt Umber with French
Ultramarine. The sky was re-wetted and the first clouds
dropped in and left to spread wet in wet. The second layer
was thinned with water and then brushed on dry to create
the broken edges of the evening clouds.

DRAMATIC LIGHT

Light effects in paintings are most effective when the light appears to come from the back of a painting. This means that the subject will be painted as a

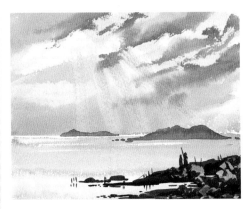

Scottish Islands

20 x 25 cm (8 x 10 in)

The sky was wetted and Cobalt Blue added. Some light areas were lifted out. The sunbursts were lifted out from the light patch at the top down to the sea. They are never parallel and always fan out. By adding the islands in opaque colour they appear to be shaded so the light falls between them.

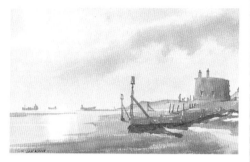

Morning Tide at Old Felixstowe, Suffolk
32 x 44 cm (12 x 17 in)
The paper was wetted and a wash of Raw Sienna added. I
removed the watery autumn sun with a tissue to create a
circle of light, then swiped the tissue down into the Sienna
below to create the light in the sea. Very pale washes were
then added with the solid objects painted in mixed greys.

silhouette, with the facing side in shade. These kinds
of study can be quite difficult when you have to
assess the strength of the foreground. Here I show
two distinct types: one with a very pale foreground
and the other very dark. They both work effectively
but notice that where the sky is pale the foreground
is pale, and where the sky is strongly painted the
foreground is dark.

PAINTING DIFFERENT SKIES

The sky above us is constantly changing as clouds form, storms brew up, and the season or time of day changes. These examples will help you to recognize different seasonal and weather effects. The light will alter as you turn to face in a new direction, so the variables are endless. You need to be able to paint not only clear summer skies but also rain clouds, stormy skies and leaden winter skies above a snow scene.

Winter skies

In winter, when there is snow on the ground, you always need a Raw Sienna base to the sky. Snow reflects a lot of light back up into the sky and shadows will be more blue or mauve.

Winter in the Dales
22 x 37 cm (8 x 14 in)
In this winter snow scene, the entire sky area was wetted with water before adding a wash of Raw Sienna.
When dry, the sky was

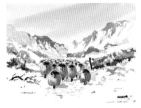

rewetted and then a wash of Raw Sienna and Alizarin Crimson was streaked across and allowed to spread to create this soft effect.

Stormy skies

For these skies, you will need to use vigorous brush strokes and stronger colours. Be prepared to work fast and decide from which direction the light is coming and also how the shadows on the ground will change before you start painting with a pale Raw Sienna wash.

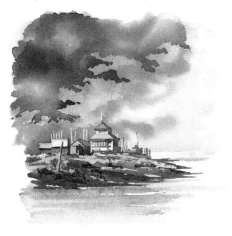

Above: The storm clouds were painted on to Cobalt Blue whilst still wet with a mix of neutral tint and French Ultramarine to give them a soft-edged rainy look.

Rainy skies

These are usually painted wet in wet, adding greys and pale browns to the clouds over the blues towards the horizon to create the impression of falling rain.

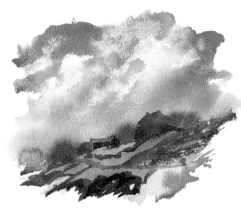

Above: In this painting of Ramsbottom rain, the sky was painted strongly with French Ultramarine and then blotted to create the light areas. Payne's Grey was added and the background was washed in wet in wet.

Summer skies with clouds

Towards mid afternoon on a hot and very still summer's day, clouds often form as the moisture rises. These skies are pale and warm and to paint them you will need Coeruleum or Manganese, washed on very thinly. Then lift out the clouds, making them progressively smaller as they recede. Shadows can be very pale; make them with a touch of Burnt Umber mixed with the sky colour. Test the colour first on a scrap of paper and let it dry so you know how dark it will look. When dry, a wash of Raw Sienna will complete the feeling of warm humidity.

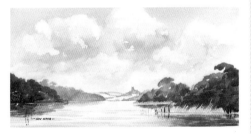

Oby, Norfolk
21 x 41 cm (8 x 16 in)
For summer skies, make everything in the distance look really pale. Imagine you are looking at this through a hazy fog and then dull it accordingly.

PAINTING BACKGROUNDS

Success in any painting depends on how you treat the background. It should always be painted transparently, often with washes created from Raw or Burnt Sienna applied on top of a sky wash. A background added with an opaque wash will always leap out at you visually, thereby ruining any sense of distance or recession.

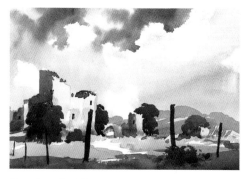

Storm Over the Ruins
22 x 37 cm (8 x 14 in)
Simple undulating tree lines show background hills perfectly. They are painted over the sky transparently and the gaps of sky add depth without detail.

CREATING TRANSPARENCY

Think of your painting like a stage set in which the background is the backdrop right at the rear. It won't have much detail and it will usually be quite pale. The brighter, stronger colours and the details will be saved for the parts of the painting that are nearer to us. To ensure the transparency works, check a colour chart – these are available from every art shop.

Colours marked with a 'T' are transparent and fine for you to use; those marked with an 'O' are opaque and aren't suitable for backgrounds. More recently, some manufacturers have started to indicate this on the tubes of paint.

The simplest way to create distance in your paintings is often a treeline, usually painted without trunks or any real definition. It is also transparent and is painted over the sky wash. Trees in the distance will never appear as dark as trees in the middle distance or foreground of your paintings. Even though they may look as dark in real life, they have to be painted paler.

FLAT AND HILLY LANDSCAPES

When you paint a flat landscape, normally there will be more layers of colour, which may be very subtle. Alternatively, some areas may be left unpainted. It will usually be one-third land and two-thirds sky whereas a hilly landscape will usually be composed of two-thirds land and one-third sky.

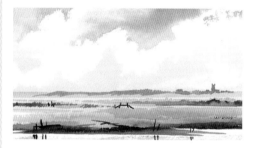

Looking Towards Winterton, Norfolk
16 x 33 cm (6 x 13 in)
In this study of a church tower seen across the marshes, each layer of colour helps to create the feeling of depth. The band of Raw Sienna across the centre and the green bank behind are both painted in the same wash. The use of slightly darker opaque washes as a contrast in the foreground gives the finished painting wonderful depth.

Farm at East Bergholt, Suffolk

15 x 20 cm (6 x 8 in)

The same technique of using Raw Sienna washes over the sky wash can be seen in this example of rolling farmland. The background is simple, understated, and pale. The tree lines are simply added in pale French Ultramarine, the farm in very thin Burnt Sienna and the roofs in more French Ultramarine. If doors, windows, cows and tractors had been added, the study would have been ruined with detail.

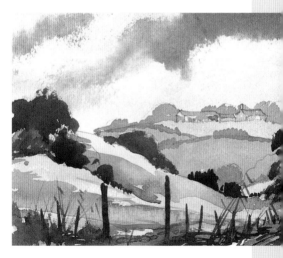

DISTANT BUILDINGS

When there is a village in the distance, you may be tempted to overpaint it. Bear in mind that the less you put into your painting, the better it will look. Less is more and you will get the maximum impact with minimal detail in many paintings.

You may feel overwhelmed by a subject because a town or a great urban sprawl is in the background. However, all you need do is take a long hard look and analyze the main shapes of colour in the architecture. Forget that it's a town; it's going to be simply a collection of coloured shapes in your painting.

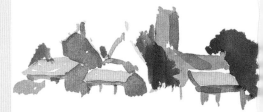

Above: This little colour sketch shows how you can paint great architecture with a touch of Burnt Sienna and some grey mixed with Burnt Umber and Cobalt Blue. When it's dry, add the shadows in a slightly stronger grey.

Shadows and trees will add the finishing touches and create the illusion of a town. My watercolour of Rye (below) demonstrates what you can achieve by keeping your painting simple and transparent. Look at the architecture; most of it was painted in simple shapes in earth colours, with the random shapes left as white paper. It looks quite solid although it is basically an abstract collection of colours.

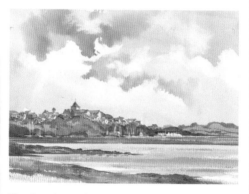

View Over the Marshes
36 x 56 cm (15 x 22 in)
Buildings viewed across water are painted with pale and transparent colours. Add the reflections with the same washes and avoid painting exact mirror images.

WOODLAND BACKGROUNDS

Trees and woodland work very effectively as backdrops to subjects with architecture, or simply to show distance and scale in open landscapes. Where the trees are close behind buildings you can afford to make them stronger than those painted in the distance. They can also have more definition even if they are painted loosely. In subjects where there are distant mountains, a solid treeline will work wonders for adding recession to a painting.

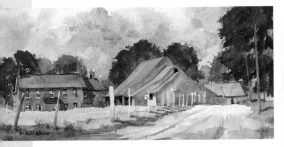

Summerhill Farm, Norfolk

18 x 38 cm (7 x 15 in)

A line of transparent trees was painted behind the farm, then more opaque trees were added with the four strongly coloured trees around the farm.

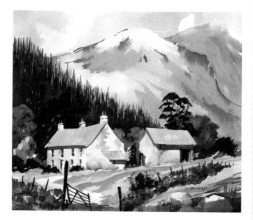

West Head Farm, Cumbria
33 x 33 cm (13 x 13 in)
Pine trees coming down a slope in the middle distance add
depth. A few solid deciduous trees around the buildings
separate the subject from the background.

TIP Even in flatter landscapes, trees can be used to create
the entire background. When you are painting pine trees,
adding a wide range of transparent and opaque greens
around any buildings will help to create a feeling of distance
and recession in your painting.

MOUNTAINS AND HILLS

Hills and mountains are ideal for showing weather conditions and also the height of the viewer in a subject. A simple range of mountains in the background to a painting can be blotted out to show mist, boats and even a lighthouse, and this is always done best on a wood-based paper. Whereas, a high foreground with hills behind creates the impression of looking up at the subject, hills that are low in the background give the feel of looking down at it. Both these approaches to the subject can be achieved through changing the eye level and thereby moving the finished height of the background.

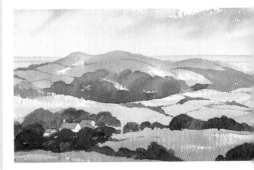

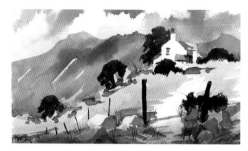

Moorland Farm

22 x 35 cm (8 x 14 in)

In this painting the subject is moved to the top third of the picture area in order to create a more dramatic study.

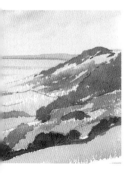

Lulworth, Dorset

32 x 48 cm (12 x 19 in)

This landscape is viewed from a high vantage point. The background hills are kept low and the sky is brought down behind. The layers of trees get progressively smaller.

BACKGROUND WEATHER

The prevailing weather conditions will influence the way in which you paint the background. For instance, a soft mist can be created simply by wiping off a layer of paint. An equally effective method is to paint the background over a wet sky.

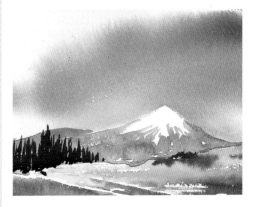

Early Snow in Perthshire
15 x 23 cm (6 x 9 in)
By drawing the mountain outline lightly in pencil you can paint the sky very wet. Leave the snow peak as dry paper before adding colours to the sky.

To paint snow on mountain tops, you can either
blot out the white areas or leave them unpainted
with the white paper showing through. If you wish
to show more detail, the mountains will need to
be more dominant.

Rain Approaching
17 x 23 cm (7 x 9 in)
This shows how to create a misty effect by laying the
background on a wet sky and tilting the board until dry.

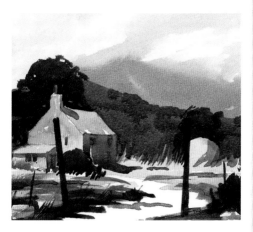

PAINTING FOREGROUNDS

The foreground is a very important part of any painting – get it right and the painting will virtually look after itself. An effective foreground will lead the eye in and create interest. It does not have to be very detailed but, more importantly, it marks the change from transparent background washes to the use of opaque foreground colours.

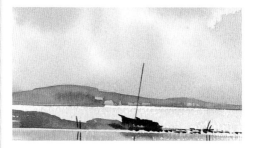

Norfolk Coastline
15 x 23 cm (6 x 9 in)
A simpler example of opacity and transparency would be hard to find. Whereas the background was painted onto the sky in a transparent wash, the foreground was added simply with opaque washes.

TWO APPROACHES

In some paintings, a foreground will work simply because of its opaque treatment whereas in others its success is due to the etching and embellishment of the opaque colours. These are two very different approaches but they are both equally effective when used in context.

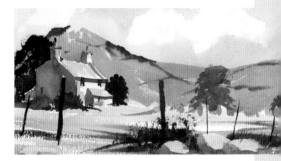

Dales Landscape
17 x 39 cm (7 x 15 in)
The foreground was created by using opaque Yellow Ochre on top of transparent Raw Sienna. This gives the landscape depth and distance. It has been enhanced by lifting out a few boulders with a credit card and adding some opaque greens and the posts.

USING THE MIDDLE DISTANCE

As the foreground will usually start at the focal plane
(see page 56) and finish at the front of your painting,
it will usually include all of the middle distance. The
content of the middle distance will vary with the type
of subject. In some cases it will be built up with light
and dark bands; in others it will only need simple
washes as the background will be more obvious.

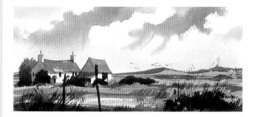

Burnham Marshes, Norfolk
16 x 35 cm (6 x 14 in)
The use of light and dark bands can be seen in this painting.
With a flat landscape, it is the only technique that works.
Some of the dark areas are painted as grasses and reeds or
simple shrubs and bushes, and the subject can be painted
in the same brushwork. This will make your painting look
cleaner. In some subjects the same effect can be achieved
simply by painting in layers of trees.

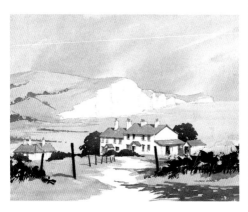

Seven Sisters, Sussex

38 x 56 cm (15 x 22 in)

Where the background is obvious, the foreground can be
painted in a couple of simple washes. The background in
this painting of the famous Sussex cliffs was painted using
transparent washes while the foreground was painted with
opaque colour. A couple of simple areas of shrubs and a
path were then added to lead the eye of the viewer into
the subject and this completed the foreground.

EMBELLISHING FOREGROUNDS

Adding some extra touches to a foreground will make it more individual. For example, it may be your style to always add some posts or a detail such as an old plough. Alternatively, you may simply get your inspiration from seeing the subject as presented to you and may want to replicate it, detail for detail. Whichever way you like to paint, the foreground should never look overworked – the simpler the better. In fact, the most effective foregrounds feature only the minimum of embellishments.

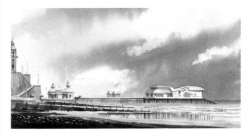

Cromer Pier, Norfolk
28 x 42 cm (11 x 17 in)
After the ebbing tide, there were wonderful reflections of the pier stantions in the wet sand. This painting shows the opportunities that a foreground can provide for painting creatively.

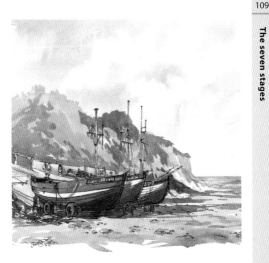

Boats at West Runton, Norfolk
28 x 28 cm (11 x 11 in)
I painted the boats, beach and cliff in loose washes and used
ink to redefine the main subject. A few pebbles were added
to the beach and picked out when adding the shadows. This
simple approach makes the foreground work well and is
worth trying when the subject is almost a foreground.

PEBBLES

The simpler and bolder your treatment of a foreground, the better it will work. For some subjects, a simple, unembellished approach creates a better foreground, but sometimes a simple wash or two won't be enough and I resort to adding pebbled paths or grasses and reeds. They look difficult to paint but are easy if you use an etching, masking or opaque colour technique. Here are some step-by-step examples.

1 For light pebbles on a dark path, mask their shapes with some masking fluid first. When dry, add some dark colour over the path.

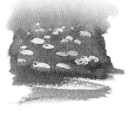

2 Make pebbles look wet by painting a pale wash of Cobalt Blue over the path after you have removed the masking fluid.

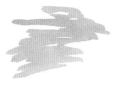

1 A wash of Raw Sienna will mark the path shape. Use horizontal, not vertical, brush strokes across the foreground.

2 Add some Yellow Ochre and Burnt Sienna to the area nearest to you to create your opacity.

3 Whilst wet, etch the pebbles with a brush handle, making the marks progressively smaller as they recede into the distance.

4 Finally, add a wash of darker colour over the immediate foreground to make the pebbles appear even stronger.

REEDS AND GRASSES

There are three basic methods of painting grasses and reeds in the foreground of a picture as demonstrated here. Deciding which method you are going to use will depend on the type of subject you are painting.

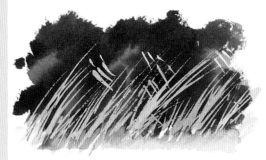

Above: Light reeds against a dark middle ground can be very dramatic. Wash in the greens for the reeds first, then let this dry well and paint the reeds with masking fluid. This enables you to keep the light grasses. When the darker middle distance greens are added, the reeds will appear as if by magic when the masking is removed.

Above: In light areas, such as cornfields, add a few simple washes in horizontal bands, the colour changing only slightly between them. Etch with a brush handle to give the effect of larger expanses of grasses.

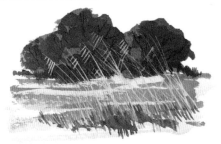

Above: Mix opaque white with Yellow Ochre to add reeds to the immediate foreground with a rigger. Practise this before you attempt it in a finished painting.

OTHER FOREGROUND FEATURES

Obviously, we cannot cover every type of foreground you may need, but here are some more examples to help you interpret what you see. Whatever you try to include, remember that simplifying a foreground and making it bold is always the best approach. Fussy, overworked foreground details can spoil a painting. If the foreground in front of you is very busy, consider how you can make it simpler and which items you need to include – three posts will often look far better than ten. Alternatively, if there is nothing obvious in the foreground, can you borrow something from elsewhere to make it more interesting?

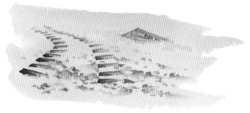

Above: A beach can be enhanced by the addition of an old fish box and a tractor track. Etch in a few pebbles and the effect is brilliant. It can also be used to lead the eye into the painting.

The most difficult of foregrounds are those where you need to show perspective; this is often in open farmland subjects. Whatever the ruts or crops are actually doing, you may need to change their direction so that they lead the viewer's eye into the painting. Ruts or crops crossing a foreground will ruin the sense of distance that you are trying to create.

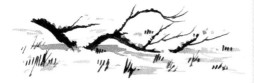

Above: Snow covers most features in a landscape, but an old tree trunk lying on the ground will still be seen even if it is partly covered in snow. These are the details to look for.

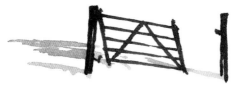

Above: I often use an old gate in my paintings but remember to open it or it will stop the eye entering the painting. It looks timeless if it hangs off its hinges.

THE MAIN SUBJECT

There is a subject everywhere so why is it so difficult to identify what we want to paint? Painters are natural observers, and the more we paint, the more we see. Training ourselves to look helps us to find a subject or, as my father put it, 'Learn to look and the subjects will look after themselves'.

LANDSCAPES

All landscapes vary enormously in their style and content – for example, they may be flat, hilly, mountainous or even a seascape. When looking at a potential landscape as a subject for your painting, the best advice I can give you is to look at the subject, think about it and then plan your picture carefully. A good way to do this is by sketching it first. Only then will you fully understand your subject.

When you are planning a landscape, always remember the rule of thirds (see page 52) and never place the subject right in the centre of your painting. Decide whether it looks best a third of the way up or down, or a third of the way in from the left or right. Where you position the subject will dramatically affect the impact and mood of the finished painting.

Broadland Pumpmill
15 x 20 cm (6 x 8 in)

With the mill dominating this painting, a simple sky and background were washed in first transparently. The mill and reeds were painted in opaque colours afterwards when the background was dry.

A more simple subject than this picture of an estuary in the early morning light (below) would be harder to find but it still needs planning. For instance, where will the horizon be? Where will the change from

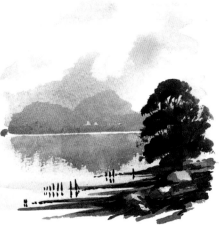

Orwell Estuary
16 x 29 cm (6 x 11 in)
Early morning light, a few distant trees and the view across the estuary. I looked straight across the estuary rather than down into it to create the best sense of distance.

transparent to opaque colour take place? What will create the best sense of distance? You need to ask yourself these questions before you paint.

The painting of St Bennet's Abbey (below) has an obvious subject. The background and foreground are easy to see and plan and are defined by the sky, which is painted down behind the abbey.

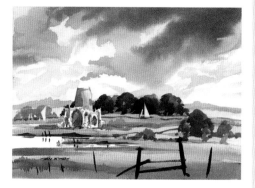

St Bennet's Abbey, Norfolk
24 x 32 cm (9 x 12 in)
You can easily see where the sky wash came down to in this study, creating the foreground and background areas. The sails in the distance were lifted out with a stencil and sponge.

BUILDINGS

Architectural subjects present many possibilities. The subject can contain buildings or the architecture can actually be the subject. Normally where you place the building(s) will be the deciding factor. If the subject is positioned quite large in the foreground, you have the opportunity to add more detail and concentrate on the architecture itself. Consequently, there will be less detail in the background.

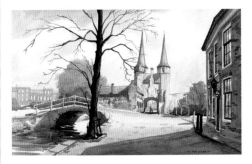

Ouestgate, Delft, Holland

38 x 56 cm (15 x 22 in)

By placing this mediaeval town gate in the middle distance, it draws the viewer's eye past the tree and bridge into the archway itself. A simply suggested background creates depth.

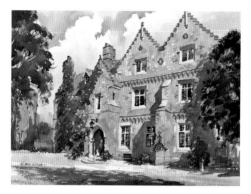

Welle Manor, Norfolk
38 x 56 cm (15 x 22 in)
Here the architecture itself is the subject. When you paint a building as close as this, you can make full use of your skills at painting details. Keep your background to an absolute minimum with this type of watercolour.

However, if the building is placed in the background, the way in which you treat it will be far simpler. This does not mean that it will be any easier to paint so don't use this as your rationale when making a decision. At the planning stage, ask yourself how you want to paint it and sketch it out both ways if necessary to see which approach looks better.

ARCHWAYS

An archway can add interest to your painting and will create a sense of depth. Not only will it lead the viewer's eye into a picture but it will also suggest a world beyond the immediate foreground. It can frame the subject or become the subject of the painting. It is advisable to make a rough sketch first to plan out your painting and get the perspective right.

Right: Often the best way to paint a complex subject like this is to paint in areas of colour and draw into it with a watersoluble pencil. It keeps the subject simple and achievable.

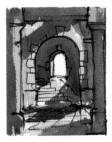

Opposite: Using an arch to frame the subject can give a study wonderful depth. I painted this in situ with a watersoluble ink pen for the drawing and then washed it out using a No. 8 brush with water. The colour was added from a very limited palette, and what an effect! This style can make architecture real fun to draw and paint.

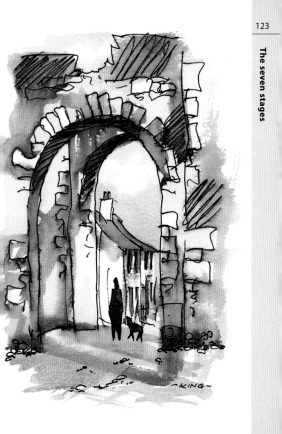

PAINTING TREES

Like every watercolour painter I have ever met, I too
had a problem with trees when I began painting.
Initially I avoided them but eventually I had to paint
them and I soon realized that they are not nearly so
difficult as they first appear and that there are some
very simple techniques to help you.

PLACING TREES

When you feel confident about painting trees you will
have gained a whole new vocabulary to paint with.
Trees can make or break a painting but not, as you
imagine, because they look awful but more by where
you place and how you use them.

The illustrated examples opposite of a simple farm
with some haystacks show you just what trees can
do in a picture. Why not try this yourself. Take some
traces of the original drawing, then paint a simple
sky, add a background and have fun experimenting.
Vary the strengths of the greens and the relative
sizes of the trees. You will soon discover that the
effects of depth will vary enormously.

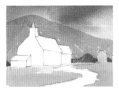

1 Painting a few simple background trees helps to separate the middle ground from the background hills.

2 An opaque tree placed behind the farm brings the farm forward. The bush in front of the haystack sends it back.

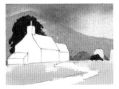

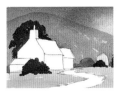

3 A bush painted in front of the farm brings the foreground forward. Another bush behind the other haystack makes it appear nearer.

4 Finally, a couple of gorse brushes in the foreground add interest and bring the foreground well forward.

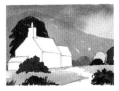

PAINTING DISTANT TREES

Painting background trees is easier if you create a line to sit them on. The colours are pale and transparent, usually paler than they appear in reality. Trees that are opaque or too dark will jump out at you and not recede effectively. If the background is flat, start with a flat broken line. If it is undulating, the line should follow the landscape. Using the edge of a brush, add the foliage down to the line by simply dragging the brush downwards – use the edge, not the point.

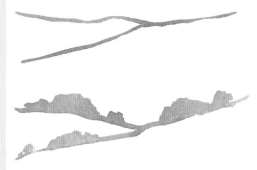

Above: You can use this same technique to show fields and hedges in the back of a painting. Keep these very simple.

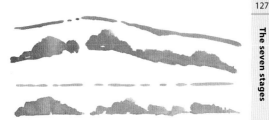

Above: Middle-distance trees are painted using the same method, but the colour can be made more opaque by adding some Yellow Ochre.

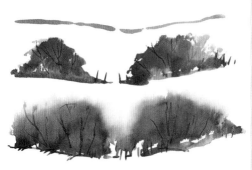

Above: If you need a misty effect, such as you would see in winter, simply wet the paper above your line before painting the trees in. Tilt the board upright and you will have a misty outline effect.

PAINTING WOODLAND TREES

Solid forests are a challenge and may be impossible to paint in watercolour so stick to subjects that have woodland as a backdrop or trees with gaps between them as a foreground. The problem is keeping our light which comes from the white paper. A mass of forest becomes muddy quickly and loses its light.

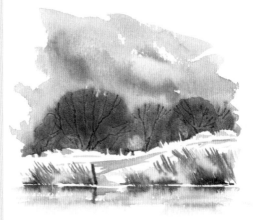

Above: The treeline was painted over the wet sky to give a soft edge. The trunks of the trees were etched in with a brush handle.

You need a variety of greens to paint trees effectively, usually made by mixing earth colours and blues and greens but never with greens straight from the tube. These always look very acidic and are not suitable for deciduous trees. Summer trees look better with gaps left in the foliage to look through to the background; winter trees are more effective with a foreground and painted wet in wet against a background sky.

Trees in recession

Often you will see a row of trees that is painted dark on light. The dark trees or hedges are painted first, leaving gaps, and when dry the lighter tree colours are painted in between. All this can be overpainted with additional greens later. This technique will give you a good sense of recession.

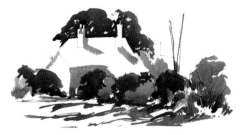

Above: You can see this technique used in the hedgerow leading the eye into this little watercolour sketch.

DIFFERENT TYPES OF TREE

There are so many species of tree that all we can do as painters is to create impressions of them in our paintings. Leave the serious study of tree forms to the arbriologists. They do, however, fall into two most noticeable types: deciduous and coniferous, with many varieties of each, and further variations according to the season.

Coniferous trees

These are by far the hardest trees to paint. The example shown of painting a pine forest is worth trying to master as you will see this fairly often and can

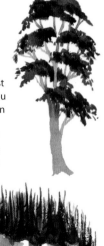

Right: See how the top branches of this Scots pine actually start halfway down the tree, and the foliage looks suspended in them.

Right: Distant coniferous trees look better if you make them appear to sit on rocky ground. Don't try to paint individual trees.

use it to separate middle grounds from foregrounds. The light trees in the background are painted first, the darker tree forms added later.

Deciduous trees

These are by far the most common trees and, incidentally, the easiest to paint. Each tree has a different overall shape, colour and pattern to its branch construction. Below are three very typical tree shapes. The pattern of the branches in winter is shown together with their summer foliage which you can create with the edge of your brush. There is not room here to show all the deciduous trees you will see so use sketches and photographs for your own reference to paint from when you cannot get outside.

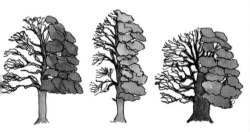

Above: These illustrations of typical deciduous tree shapes show their winter skeleton and their summer foliage.

SEASONAL TREES

The techniques that are used for painting trees in the distance do not really vary with the changing seasons, apart from the change in the colour of the foliage. The extra detail you see and will want to show with foreground trees requires two very different approaches: one for winter and one for summer. To most novice painters, trees often present a huge problem. However, with a bit of observation and practice you will soon learn how to make the most of them.

Few landscapes come without trees and the following exercises show you how to create them simply but effectively, no matter what the season. The more practice you get at painting different trees, the better and easier it will become.

Summer trees

Look carefully at a few trees before you start to paint. You can see that the foliage on many of them looks rather like a field mushroom which has been cut through in half. To create effective trees, you can try using the basic shape shown opposite. You can also experiment with some different tree shapes. The colour of the leaves will vary throughout the summer months so you must expect to have to mix plenty of greens.

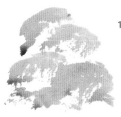

1 Mix a wash of Raw Sienna with Hookers Green. Create an interlocking area of mushroom shapes with a brush on its heel.

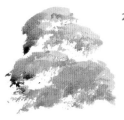

2 Decide where your light is coming from. Add French Ultramarine to the wash and then paint in the shadow sides and underneath the foliage. This is best done before the paint is totally dry.

3 Add the trunk and branches with a wash of Burnt Umber, leaving gaps so the foliage is in front of the trunks. While wet, add a touch of French Ultramarine to vary the colour. Add the shadows with the same wash.

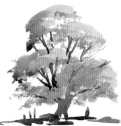

Winter trees

Winter trees can often be quite a challenge for the beginner to paint, not least because all the branches need painting in. The method I always use is to paint the main trunk and branches first, and then I pencil in the overall tree shape and mark the centre of this with a cross. Don't worry about all the pencil lines – they are easy to erase when the painting is dry.

A friend of mine who is an arborist thinks that these trees are wrong but, as I tell him, I sell more of them than he does!

TIP You only ever use the tip of the rigger, and keeping it at even pressure is difficult. To overcome this, use your knuckle as a support so the pressure and line remain constant. If your lines appear uneven, check whether the point has become worn; if so, save this particular brush for putting on masking fluid. If you're not used to using a rigger, then try it out on a scrap of paper first. If you find it difficult, turn it upside-down, especially if you are left-handed. The bottom branches will always turn up at the ends.

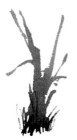

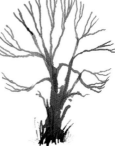

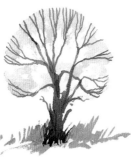

1 Create your framework using Burnt Umber. Add a little Prussian Blue and paint the ivy. Next add a patch of dead grass with Yellow Ochre and enjoy a quick etch with your brush handle.

2 Draw in the tree shape; mark the centre with a cross. Use a rigger to paint the branches, starting at the cross and fanning out to end on the pencil line.

3 When it is dry, use a mop on its edge to add a little dirty water for the small areas of twigs.

ADDING THE DETAILS

In many respects, this is a misnomer to painters. The word 'detail' suggests lots of lines and fuss but nothing could be further from the truth. Your painting should not look like a photograph and the detail is often an illusion!

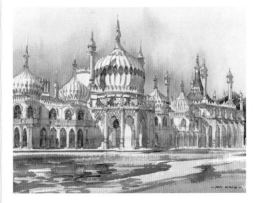

Royal Pavilion, Brighton
38 x 56 cm (15 x 22 in)
For such a complex building, the detail is minimal. The overall effect is created with shadows.

LIGHT AND SHADOWS

Most beginners learn to paint from photographs and strive to make their paintings look as much like them as possible, but the trick with detail in a successful painting is not to paint any; it should be only a suggestion of what is there. The easiest way to do this is to use shadows to suggest shapes and forms on simple colour bases.

Try painting lots of simple coloured shapes and adding shadows to them or around them. You will soon discover that a great deal can be achieved with very simple brushwork. The more you do, the more skilful you will become!

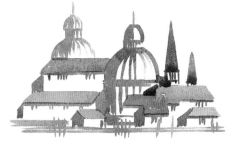

Above: You can create buildings from coloured shapes. A few simple roof shapes can look spectacular.

BRICKS AND STONE

Buildings always present the painter with a challenge. They may be constructed from thousands of bricks and stones or, worse still, from concrete. I tell my students that although there may be 230,017 bricks in a wall, you can get away with painting only 40 of them. Not only will it look better but you might have it finished before supper!

1 When painting brickwork, put a basic wash of colour over the wall.

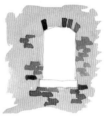

2 Paint stronger coloured shapes of bricks in random patterns over this.

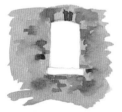

3 Simply tease them around with a damp brush, and they will look like perfect brickwork.

Stonework

If the stonework is trimmed, paint it like the brickwork; if it is loose, as in a dry stone wall, paint it as shown in the example below.

1 Paint a coloured base for the wall, making it darker at the bottom.

2 Etch the stones into the wall with a brush handle (see page 30).

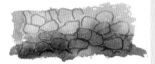

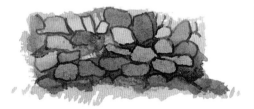

3 A few darker areas of shadow will help to create a perfect stone wall.

WINDOWS

Painting buildings will always involve doorways and windows. These can be quite tricky to paint so practise drawing a few first to learn how they look and also how their shapes change when they are

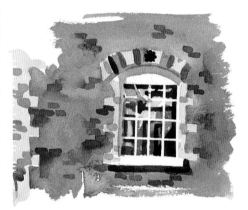

Above: The timbers in the window frame were masked out as white. The basic blue of the glass was added and, when dry, the reflections were painted in. You will see all kinds of shapes reflected in glass, and it is often best to look through sunglasses to help you identify them.

viewed from various angles. There is no such thing as a typical window, but they do all have one thing in common – glass – and this must be painted well in order to work effectively.

Sash windows

In a sash window, the top section is usually in front of the bottom one. When painting this, show the different thicknesses of the timbers, and how the glazing bars are offset in the lower window.

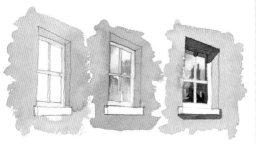

Above: With windows, the easiest way to keep the glazing bars is to mask them with fluid. The glass can then be painted simply but boldly with washes over washes. All you are painting is the reflection in the glass itself. Remove the masking before adding the shadows!

DOORWAYS

Even a plain door can enhance a painting. You can
make it whatever you like – old or new and bright,
with or without steps or with a boot cleaner, perhaps.

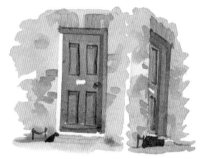

Above: When you look at a door straight on, you will see the
door frame all around it. However, when it is viewed from
an angle, the first part of the door will usually disappear
behind the brickwork.

TIP Polished metals and glass reflect light and other objects.
Outdoors, they reflect their environment; indoors, place a few
bright strips of coloured paper nearby to make reflections
appear in them. Add a basic wash colour (blue for glass, pale
orange for brass) and paint the reflections over this.

Larger doorways

Try experimenting with various types of doorways; practice will make perfect. The illustration below shows what can be achieved with a pair of large doors. Garage, workshop or barn doors all offer an opportunity to open them up and play around inside – an effective way of attracting the viewer's eye.

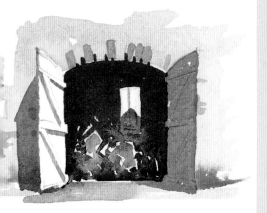

Above: A window at the back creates light; some loose, coloured areas become a piece of farm machinery, enabling you to make better use of the shadows.

TEXTURES AND MATERIALS

You can have fun experimenting with painting a variety of surfaces and textures. There is no fixed way of doing this and you may need to plan a wash over another wash, using masking fluid or candle wax (see page 33). Another technique is to lay a wash, then cover it in cling film for a cracked effect. Try out different ideas, keeping all your workings for future reference. What seems less effective today may actually become a way of creating another effect in the future.

Painting rust

To make materials and buildings look old and moody, add some rust. It's very simple and you will soon master the technique shown below.

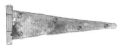

1 Paint the metal first in a rusty mix of colours. Don't worry if the odd watermark appears.

2 Add some candle wax to this, then lay the darker colour over it. The wax will resist the paint and the metal will look effectively rusty.

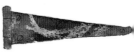

Wood grain

You can see the grain pattern in wood when it is cut and planed. There are three basic ways of creating the effect of wood grain as shown below.

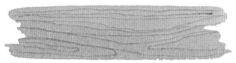

Above: Etch the grain into the wet paint with a brush handle.

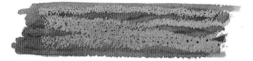

Above: Apply some wax over the first wash, and then add a second wash over the wax.

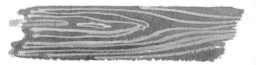

Above: Apply masking fluid over the first wash, when dry. Then add a second wash to reveal the lighter wash underneath. This gives a more controlled effect.

OTHER WAYS TO ADD DETAILS

Details can be added at virtually any stage, especially by etching into wet paint. However, this must be done immediately as re-wetting and trying to etch doesn't work. Details can be added in Stage 6 (see page 63), or when everything is dry, using ink, pencil or pastel.

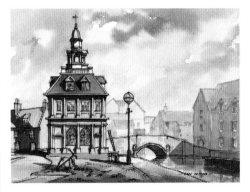

The Customs House, King's Lynn
28 x 38 cm (11 x 15 in)
This atmospheric study is further enhanced by painting the subject simply and adding the foreground buildings and details in ink over the watercolour. The background is left undefined, thereby creating a sense of distance and depth.

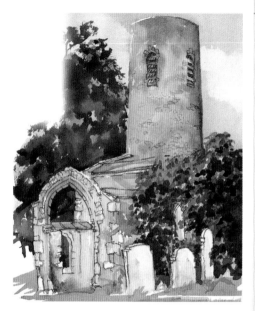

Haute Bois Church, Norfolk
30 x 20 cm (12 x 8 in)
A ruined church offers plenty of textures and forms. I painted the stonework, then etched in the wet tower and painted the porchway, walls and gravestones. I drew into these whilst they were still wet with a water-soluble pencil.

CREATING SHADOWS

There are many accepted ways of shading a painting but no set rules. It all depends on how you structure your painting. Because I always use my seven-stage method, my shadows go in last. This way, the edges of the shadows don't get washed out and remain sharp. For a watercolour to look sunny and bright, you need sharp-edged shadows.

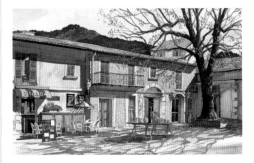

Place de Valldemossa, Majorca
28 x 38 cm (11 x 15 in)
Shadows from trees across a street or alley help to create drama and distance in your paintings as well as showing the direction of the light.

PLACING SHADOWS

Shadows make your paintings three-dimensional. In landscapes, the main light source always comes from one direction so make sure that you place all the shadows at the same time. In this way, a wash of consistent strength and hue can be used.

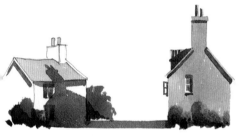

Above: Shadows can make or break a painting. To discover where best to place shadows, you need to study many different buildings on sunny days and then you will become knowledgeable. Shadows are very effective when crossing space and falling onto other buildings. Notice how the shadow of the house on the right bends over the walls and the roof of the building on the left.

SHADOWS IN LANDSCAPES

As with buildings, shadows in landscapes increase the
recession effect. Any device that allows you to create
light and dark bands across a foreground is worth using.
On many occasions, I change the light direction
completely to make this happen. Very often the
shadows in a landscape will be created by trees, and
these shadows will vary with the season.

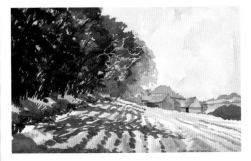

Norfolk Farmland
28 x 38 cm (11 x 15 in)
The light here is coming from the north but I wanted a warm
feel to the foreground to create depth so I moved the sun
round 180 degrees. The shadows falling down the banks and
into the ruts help create the flow of the landscape.

Right: Shadows cast by winter trees are usually quite pale as lots of light comes through the trees. They are always linear as they repeat the shapes of the branches. Always shade the shadows of the branches on the trunk.

Right: Shadows under summer trees can be very dark. This shadow extends beyond the tree and is best painted all in one go with nervous lines wet into wet. Never go back into the wet paint to touch it up or you will have ugly watermarks.

CHANGING DIRECTION

Planning a painting works and you can take it a stage further by changing the direction of the light. Using your original drawing, trace it through a few times onto some cartridge paper and see how placing the shadows in different positions will make or break it. I have included some quick sketches to show how changing the light can transform a simple street. I have added extra trees to make more shadows available or create counterchange.

Whenever you paint a street or lane, try out this little exercise. Indicate the shadows in pencil if wished. You can learn a lot about light from these studies. They will help you determine the way that shadows fall from and on to roofs and buildings, and that in itself will save you from many a looming disaster.

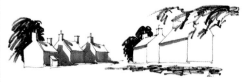

Above: The light appears to come from the left front of the painting. It leaves the fronts of the three cottages dark and the two on the right light. Placing a large tree behind the two light walls and a tree in the front at the right enhances the view.

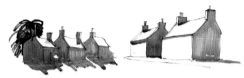

Above: Shading the painting from the left from the back takes most of the light out of it. The shadows don't work well and the counterchange is not effective.

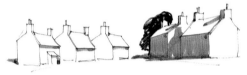

Above: The light coming from the right front does little to show the forms of the cottages. Chimney stacks get lost, and the overall subject looks flat. Shadows help to create a three-dimensional painting.

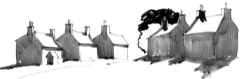

Above: With the light from the right back the two nearest cottages become dark and much of the light in the painting is lost. The cottages on the left look interesting and brighten the painting but they don't work as well as the first study.

OTHER TYPES OF SHADOW

Shading is usually straightforward, but there are some occasions when the colour of the shadows will be affected by the weather or the subject, especially when large areas of white remain in a painting. Mills, weatherboarding, windmills, lighthouses and snow scenes all require a change from normal shading.

Church Street, Rye, Sussex

38 x 56 cm (15 x 22 in)

This shows how reflected light lightens a wall in the shade. The shadows are as you would expect except for the wall on the right which is almost as light as the wall on the other side of the street. I added a very weak wash of French Ultramarine to cool it slightly without losing any of the reflected light.

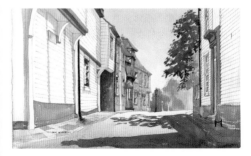

The mix should be mauve rather than the landscape greys of Burnt Umber and French Ultramarine, or the architectural greys: Burnt Sienna and French Ultramarine. A grey shadow across white looks dirty and flat but a mauve shadow gives warmth and light. Sometimes the white in the subject will reflect light back and this will change the appearance of the darks. In snow scenes, there will always be some Raw Sienna in the sky as the light is reflected back from the snow.

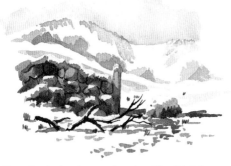

Above: For shadows in snow, draw the subject lightly in pencil, then imagine the surfaces where the snow would settle. Leave the ground as white paper and use masking fluid to mask the snow on solid forms. Paint as normal and when dry remove the masking. The magic happens when the shadows are added.

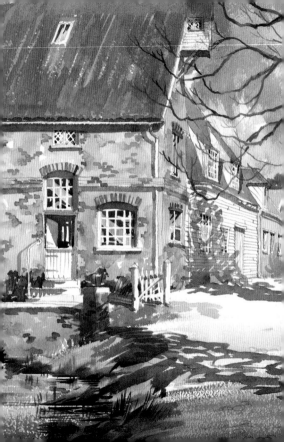

PART THREE

The next step

In the previous sections of this book, we have been looking at how to develop your basic watercolour techniques. By now, you will realize that good painting needs to be structured. I have spoken about colour being your alphabet and brushwork your language, but now it's time to get painting and add some slightly more difficult subjects to your repertoire – water, always a challenge, and figures, which provide interest in a picture.

Flatford Mill, Suffolk
38 x 38 cm (15 x 15 in)
I planned my painting to look up the lane rather than focusing on the mill. This enabled me to contrast the earth colours in the architecture with the deep greens of the hedgerow and pool. The morning light casts shadows across the lane to create depth.

PAINTING WATER

Learning to paint water, moving or still, enables you to expand your range of subjects to include virtually any landscape. Still water, such as estuaries, lakes and puddles, may be painted or even left as white paper if you are close to the subject, but you will usually have to paint moving water, too, including waterfalls, rivers, streams and the sea.

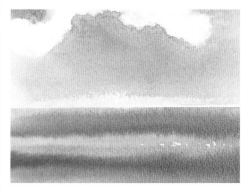

Above: Wet the area you want to be light, then wash some blue all over what will be the water. The same applies if you are painting the water light and adding a dark streak.

HOW BEST TO PAINT IT

The horizon behind the water must be flat. Paint the sky, ensuring a level base by using masking tape or painting along a line drawn across the paper. Leave a gap between water and sky to separate them. Distance is created with dark and light bands. Painting these at the normal angle will cause the bands to sag but turning your board on its side will make any runs vertical and, when returned to the upright position, horizontal.

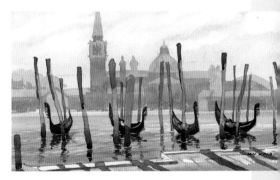

Maggiore St Giorgio, Venice
19 x 38 cm (7 x 15 in)
Looking into the sun, the only reflections here are from the gondolas in the foreground.

PAINTING THE WATER OR NOT?

Whatever goes above goes below, or does it? Let's look at two watercolours which both use the same drag technique for creating reflections. In one, Autumn on the Broads, the water is painted. However, in the other picture, Thornham Sluice, where the viewer is much closer to the water's edge, the water is left as white paper to create a brilliant, glossy feel. The appearance of the light in the water is strikingly different in each of these paintings.

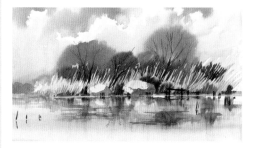

Autumn on the Broads
38 x 56 cm (15 x 22 in)
A wet area was brushed through the centre, then a wash of Cobalt Blue was added, and a pale wash of French Ultramarine to the foreground.

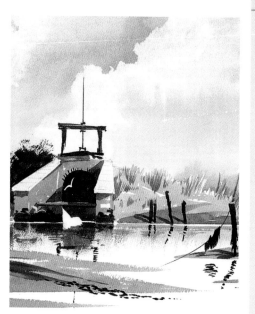

Thornham Sluice

37 x 30 cm (15 x 12 in)

The sky was painted to the top of the banks. Pale greens make up the distance. Reflections were added by dragging down the paint with a thumb.

REFLECTIONS IN STILL WATER

One of the simplest ways of adding reflections in still water is to simply paint the colour on and then drag it down with the edge of your thumb.

Masking fluid can be used to save colour as well as white paper. However, always make sure that the paint is dry before adding each layer of fluid or it will soak into the paper and you won't be able to remove it.

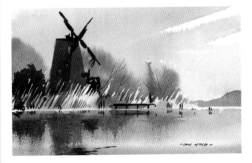

A Broadland Windmill
16 x 26 cm (6 x 10 in)
This shows the effect of a wet streak through water painted on its edge. If this had been allowed to run down and sagged, the effect would have been ruined.

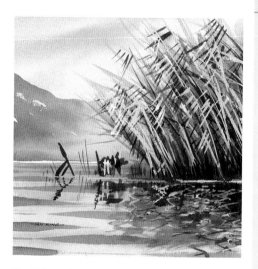

The Welle Creek, Cambridgeshire
34 x 32 cm (13 x 12 in)
I painted the reeds in a block of pale Raw Sienna with a little in the water below. When dry, I painted some of the reeds with masking fluid, using an old rigger, and added some reflections, then left it to dry. In this way, I built up three layers of different colour reeds, protected by the masking fluid.

PAINTING PUDDLES

Usually the water in puddles is left uncoloured as white paper. This is because the detailed part of the painting is usually quite close to you and therefore the water needs to stay bright in order to work well.

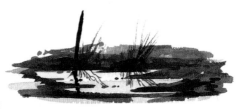

Above: This simple study shows how a mirror image of the grasses is reflected in the puddle below them.

The far edge of each puddle must be flat or it will appear to be going uphill. As water finds its own level this would look wrong, even when viewed from above. Reflections are a 'mirror image' of what is above the puddles. Objects that lean to the left in reality will lean to the left in the reflection, and vice versa. Usually there is no need to drag the reflections; just paint them in accurately with sharp edges. Before you start painting, make a pencil sketch to indicate where the puddles are going to lie, making sure their far sides are flat.

Right: It is only the sky that is reflected in these puddles in a ploughed field. The background is too far away and not sufficiently detailed to be reflected.

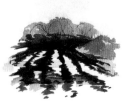

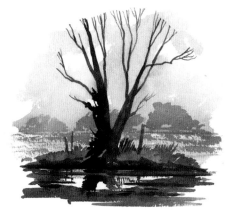

Above: This atmospheric study was made at the entrance to some fields near my studio. It had recently rained, everything was wet and the puddles were quite full.

PAINTING RIVERS

In moving water, the reflected light also moves, affecting the sky, solid masses, such as bridges, and natural objects, such as grasses and trees. There will be no visual mirror image – merely an array of colours blended together. Moving water is often better painted quickly as in the examples shown here of the same subject. The view below is a classic watercolour while opposite is an ink and watercolour treatment.

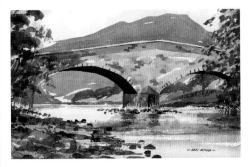

Ouse Bridge in Summer
22 x 37 cm (8 x 14 in)
The reflections of the bridge and trees were painted loosely to create the sense of movement in the river below. Candle wax was drawn across to create the ripples.

I sketched in the bridge, arches, banks and some of the main trees and boulders with ink, then painted the background hills and trees loosely, adding some of this colour in wavy stripes to the reflections. The earth colours of the bridge were also used in its reflection. There was still lots of white paper left in the water and I managed to keep a lot of it as I painted the sky in pale Cobalt Blue and added stripes of it to the water.

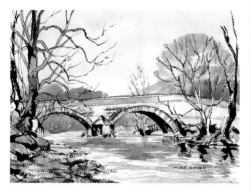

Ouse Bridge in Winter
26 x 35 cm (10 x 14 in)
To add vibrancy and contrast, black ink is used to define the arches of the bridge and the tree trunks.

STREAMS AND WATERFALLS

Streams and waterfalls are very much a 'sketchy' type of subject; the looser the treatment the better and the more effective the finished painting will be. In the example shown opposite, I sketched the subject and then re-drew it again simply to give me a good understanding of what I was trying to paint.

I masked the white areas I needed with masking fluid, washed all the colour areas in, outlined them in pencil, then masked my light areas again and added the darks. Without a clear understanding of the subject, this would have been a nightmare lack of planning. You only need to look at some of Turner's working sketches to see this, but remember that your sketch is only a working drawing – not a work of art!

After transferring your sketch to watercolour paper, mask out the whites. Do this minimally as too much masking fluid can actually spoil a painting. Only

TIP When painting ripples, use a straight edge held slightly off your paper. Run the brush along the straight edge, varying the pressure to create thick and thin lines. Try this out on a scrap of paper first. I always use a No. 8 round brush; it may look big but it works well.

remove the masking fluid when the painting is dry and before you add the shadows. You can add a little sparkle to the waterfall, if wished, by lifting out some vertical lights with a sharp blade.

Using the technique of drawing over your paint will make a subject like this not only easier but usually more fresh when completed.

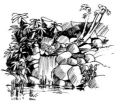

The Waterfall at Higham Hall

19 x 22 cm (7 x 8 in)

The small sketch (right) shows the detail that I needed to be able to plan the watercolour.

Making a sketch will force you to look closely at your subject; observation is more important than quality here.

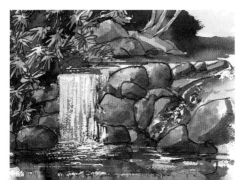

CREATING WAVES AND SEA

Before painting the sea, look closely at it, and study some paintings or photographs as a still reference to enable you to observe the shapes of the waves properly. Essentially they are white spaces with shadows and can be created using a wide variety of techniques. You can lift them out, using some tissue in wet paint or draw around them and painting around the white areas to keep the shapes intact.

Alternatively, mask them out with masking fluid or add them in body colour. If lifting out, always use a wood pulp paper, such as Bockingford. Plan the waves carefully – they are all you have to show distance – and try to keep them horizontal. For the finer spray, scratch it out with a sharp blade once dry.

As an exercise, draw a simple groyne. Mark in your horizon, add a simple sky and then paint in the sea, painting around the white waves or blotting them

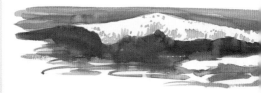

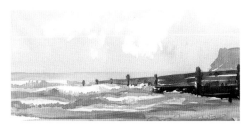

A Beach and Groyne
15 x 37 cm (6 x 14 in)
The waves were created by painting around them and then
picking out the spray with a knife.

out. Add a simple background of cliffs and a beach
with a combination of earth colours. Slightly cover
the sand at the front with the sea wash. Etch this with
a brush handle to form pebbles. Paint in the groyne
with differing strengths of Burnt Umber and add
some seaweed. Add the shadows to the waves with
a mixture of Burnt Umber and Cobalt Blue.

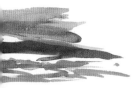

Left: Use Raw Sienna and
French Ultramarine for the
sea. Paint around the whites
of the waves or blot with
tissue. Add darker colour to
the water under the waves.

Hunstanton Beach and Cliffs

38 x 56 cm (15 x 22 in)
Before I started to paint, I sketched out this picture and used candle wax to create broken white areas in the foreground for the waves and foam. The crests of the waves were added using an old rigger with some masking fluid. The sea was painted over the top with a mix of Raw Sienna and Cobalt Blue. The board was turned round 90 degrees and the sea was dragged up vertically with a damp brush over some of the beach to create wet sand. A small light gap was left under each boulder and shadows were added under the wave crests.

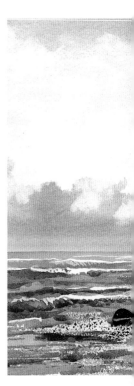

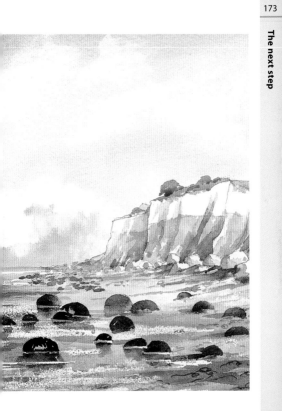

PAINTING BOATS

As tides flow in and out, the water in a harbour is never still. There's always movement and you can show this by painting the reflections in shapes that are similar to those of the boats themselves; it's as simple as that. The more the shapes move, the more the reflections will appear to move. Here's a basic step-by-step guide to painting a boat and its reflection.

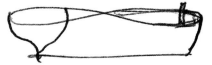

1 Start with an extended figure of eight, then add a 'wine glass' to the stern. Mark in the front and add some planks, leaving a gap in the middle.

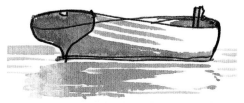

2 Paint a simple outline of the subject. Do this by brushing with a pale wash of Cobalt Blue.

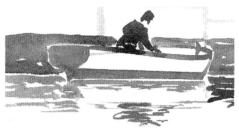

3 The water level should be a third of the way up the boat. Complete the boat and figure, adding Burnt Sienna for the stern, and Cobalt Blue at the base. Add the reflections, leaving a white gap in between.

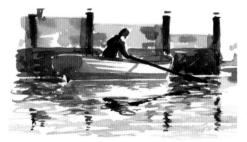

4 Indicate the jetty, adding reflections. Leave a gap for the water's edge on the wall. Paint the stones in Raw Sienna and Burnt Umber, adding reflections. Add the boat timbers, then add some wavy reflections.

DISTANT BOATS

The easiest way to show distant boats is to paint your subject, complete with its background and foreground, then make a paper stencil and lift out the features you want. Extra colour can then be added to the lifted out subjects if necessary.

Remember that a large part of a floating boat is under the water and this is how it needs to look in your paintings. If a boat has a large bow wave it is because it is ploughing through the waves. Always make a boat look as if it is floating in water and not in air.

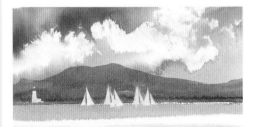

Above: The boats and lighthouse were lifted out with a stencil and damp sponge after the watercolour dried.

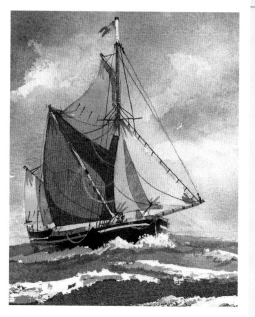

Thames Barge off Maplin

37 x 30 cm (15 x 12 in)

The sails were painted bright against a broken grey windy sky
to make the vessel look as if it is catching rays of sunlight
coming through the clouds.

FIGURES IN PAINTING

The idea of painting people can actually be quite frightening for many painters, especially novices, and this deters them from ever attempting to add the odd figure into a subject. However, as we shall see, figures can sometimes have a very beneficial effect on an otherwise quite ordinary subject.

Why add figures?

Figures can be used to show scale and depth. They can draw the viewer's eye into the back of a painting. Often it will be simply a fun subject, an attempt to paint the impossible, or what may have been dismissed as being impossible. A few figures can create a striking subject which you would never have thought possible.

Painting a town square, a railway station or a view where there are crowds is a daunting prospect, but it's the use of figures that makes those kinds of subjects achievable.

Many years ago, as a struggling art teacher, I tried to get youngsters to include figures in their paintings and, of course, they were totally intimidated. But I found a solution to painting figures that worked, and now I pass it on to you.

CREATING SIMPLE FIGURES

To create a good balanced figure, all you need to paint is an 'M' and underneath a symmetrical 'W'. Add a pair of shoulders and some hair – you do not need to fuss over faces – a pair of arms and fill in the gaps. You will have a simple figure. With practice, you can create any shape you want. As long as the Ms and Ws are in proportion it will work. You can paint them in very light paint and then add the clothing later if you wish. By altering the angles of the Ms and Ws you can even create figures in totally different poses.

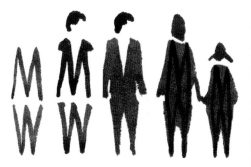

Above: From a simple M and W a huge range of figures can be created. Gaps for faces will make them face forward; solid hair shapes backward. Vary the size of the Ms and Ws for larger people!

Right: When you want figures against a background, paint the figures first in light paint. Add the background and then finish the figures so that the paint slightly overlaps. This makes the figures appear in front of the subject.

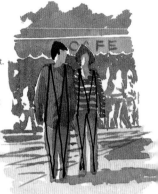

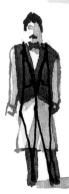

Left: Paint the M and W in very pale paint if you want to have light clothing as in the French waiter here. I have added the lines over to help you see the Ms and Ws.

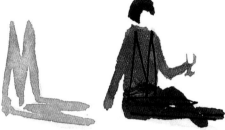

Above: By having a right angle in the M and W, a seated figure can be painted with one leg bent which will give it balance.

TIP How do you decide on whether to paint a figure or not? Heathcote has lived in my watercolour box for years. When I need to make a decision as to whether a figure would make a watercolour work better or not out he comes. By holding him in the painting I can tell immediately. This is safer than painting a figure in and hoping for the best – Heathcote is easier to remove. Keep a couple of figures handy in two different sizes: one for your backgrounds and the other for foregrounds.

USING FIGURES TO SHOW SCALE

You can use figures to add a sense of scale to your pictures. Both the arches illustrated (below) were identical in appearance until the figures were placed in them. You can see that the arch on the left becomes a grand entrance whereas the arch on the right becomes no more than a passageway.

Deciding how large a figure needs to be can be a problem but not if you adopt this simple solution. In the painting opposite I have used three identical-sized figures and have placed each one at a different level. You will soon see which figure looks correct and which ones are either too large or too small.

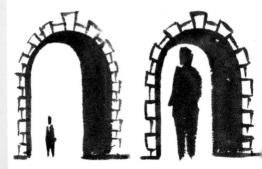

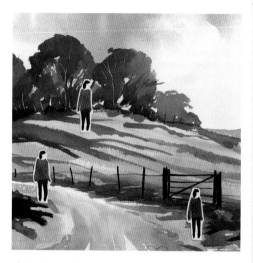

Above: It's a good idea to paint a figure on a scrap of paper, then cut around it and try placing it in different positions on your painting. Move it around and you will soon see where it looks the right size – in this case, the figure on the left.

Left: Draw the same-sized arch twice and then practise adding figures of different sizes to see how they can affect the sense of scale of the archway.

FIGURES IN A LANDSCAPE

The size of figures in a painting can also be used to indicate scale. A couple of very small figures can help to make a landscape appear larger in scale and more vast, whereas using larger figures can cause the background to appear nearer to the viewer. This is

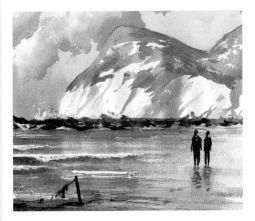

A Walk on the Beach
35 x 45 cm (14 x 18 in)
The couple strolling along the beach make the cliffs behind the seascape appear to be quite close to the viewer.

because we can all relate to the size of people and our interpretation of scale of a particular subject comes from this knowledge.

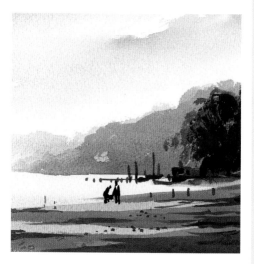

Estuary with Figures
30 x 30 cm (12 x 12 in)
The addition of two very small figures walking along the shoreline helps to make the estuary look vast in this atmospheric painting.

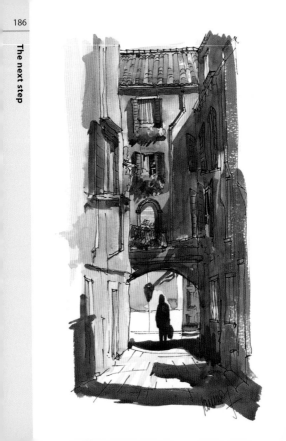

THE DYNAMIC EFFECT

Figures can add dynamism to a painting and perform several key functions. They can be used to show scale, to help draw the viewer's eye into the painting and to greatly enhance the work that is performed by shadows. They can also create the 'Giles effect', following on from that great cartoonist who always drew some extra fascinating little detail in a corner which made you look again.

We all like looking at people, especially when they are doing something, perhaps a single figure, an intimate conversation or a group activity. Whatever it is, it will add interest to your paintings. Figures always look better in the background if they are walking into the distance or stationary and conversing with each other. They will never look right if they are walking out of a background towards the viewer; it is almost as if you expect them to get nearer but they never do.

Calle del Tagiapiera, Venice
34 x 16 cm (13 x 6 in)
This quick sketch makes use of a girl entering the shadow of an arch with a light square behind. The eye is drawn into the back of the subject by the M and W figure. Without it, the subject would have had little depth or feeling. The dark figure helps create the feeling of it being hot – and it was!

FIGURES IN PERSPECTIVE

People as a subject can be a challenge and the trick is to make them appear in perspective. This, at first, may seem quite difficult but if you line all the figures up at the same point it becomes easy. The level will always be at your own eye level. Try varying the sizes of the figures across your paintings – for instance, some could be facing each other in conversation, some standing, some walking, some carrying goods or bags. Experiment with adding children to create interest, although they will be smaller and will be lined up with the feet of the nearest adult.

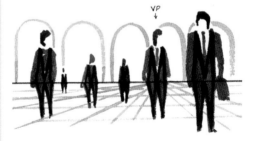

Above: Before starting to paint, always make a pencil sketch or plan out your painting, placing your figures first and then adding the background .

To paint a group of figures that looks part of a subject and works within the perspective, you simply have to paint them all with the join between the Ms and Ws at the same level. No matter what the size of the figures, they will look right in a background as long as the Ms and Ws are in proportion to each other. The view point for the perspective will always be at the same level as the point where the M and W figures join. This becomes your eye level.

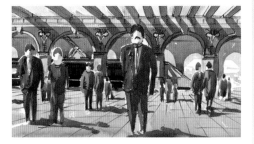

Above: In this quick watercolour of a busy railway station, the Ms and Ws were painted in a light wash with the figures' hips lining up at the same level. The eye level of the perspective is also at the same level. After painting the figures, you can add the details, background and shadows. Although painted quickly, it captures the feel of a busy railway station.

INDEX